Rastafarian Children of Solomon

"Folklorist Gerald Hausman takes us deep into the modern dreamtime of Jamaica's backwaters, enthralled by the company of living prophets and conmen, killers and saints, obeah workers and ethereal half-real creatures of the sea. They are all, as his eloquent mythlike prose reveals, the voices of the cherubim and seraphim of old."

ROGER STEFFENS,
FOUNDING EDITOR OF *THE BEAT* MAGAZINE
AND COAUTHOR OF *THE REGGAE SCRAPBOOK* AND
ONE LOVE: LIFE WITH BOB MARLEY AND THE WAILERS

Rastafarian Children of Solomon

The Legacy of the Kebra Nagast and the Path to Peace and Understanding

GERALD HAUSMAN

Bear & Company
Rochester, Vermont • Toronto, Canada

Bear & Company
One Park Street
Rochester, Vermont 05767
www.BearandCompanyBooks.com

Bear & Company is a division of Inner Traditions International

Library of Congress Cataloging-in-Publication Data
Hausman, Gerald.
  Rastafarian children of Solomon : the legacy of the Kebra Nagast and the path to
peace and understanding / Gerald Hausman.
      p. cm.
  Includes bibliographical references (p.   ) and index.
  ISBN 978-1-59143-154-1 (pbk.) — ISBN 978-1-59143-830-4 (e-book)
  1. Rastafari movement. 2. Kebra nagast—Criticism, interpretation, etc. I. Title.
  BL2532.R37H38 2013
  299.6'76—dc23

Printed and bound in the United States

10 9 8 7 6 5

Text design and layout by Brian Boynton
This book was typeset in Garamond Premier Pro with Gill Sans, Legacy Sans, and
Calligraphic 421 used as display typefaces

To send correspondence to the author of this book, mail a first-class letter to the
author c/o Inner Traditions • Bear & Company, One Park Street, Rochester, VT
05767, and we will forward the communication, or visit the author's website at
www.geraldhausman.com.

Contents

ACKNOWLEDGMENTS

It Takes a Village to Write a Book

Deep gratitude to Dr. Michael Gleeson, friend and anthropology mentor. Mike said, "First you see Jamaica, then you love it, then you marry it." He did: so thanks to him and his gracious wife Michele and his son Miggy with whom we had so many adventures with tree frogs in the night and *bufos* in the day.

My wife Lorry who is me spelled differently, and who lets me see through her eyes as she sees through mine. Mariah Fox, our daughter and constant companion in back-a-yard reasoning sessions, the artist whose paintings grace these pages and the one who took Dr. Mike's advice and married the island. Thanks, too, to Sava, her husband because blood is thicker than water. To Shai, Taj, and Anais, our Jamerican grandkids. Hannah Hausman, nicknamed "business lady" at age ten because she ran a drinks and snack store at our school, the first entrepreneur to have an ice box business that worked, made money.

Thanks to Cedella Marley who's always there to tell how it really was, not the way people imagine it but the truth of it.

Mackie McDonnough: Jamaica mentor and friend who took us to Rastafari and left us there to simmer and be. His family: Dido, Junior, Lorraine, Lorna, and Jeremy—made us welcome in their home in Highgate when our daughter Hannah lived with them. Roy McKay stuck by us through thick and thin, good times, hard times, all times: glad times.

Spreeboy, the great rememberer of early days of Rastafari, helping us with that which we would never find in books. Ernie Uton Hinds for getting us there and back and there and back again, all over the island until it was the back of our hand and the bottom of our feet. Stan (Irons) whose story is a mainstay, as he, himself, is a mainstay. Dreamy Leroy Harrow, Julie, Pansy, Candy, Mark, Merline, Michael, Miss Jenny: mainstays of our school, the ones who kept the kitchen going, the food coming, kept the cockroaches out, made our students feel at home.

Raggy Anthony Henry and his whole family: May, Doodus (Janga), Son, Michelle, Delly: without Raggy the magical long-distance swims beyond the reef never would have happened, nor the secret prowling amidst sweltering attics of Blue Harbour. Benji Oswald Brown, translator and interpreter, gone but not forgotten. Special thanks to Pansy Carlette Douglas who, with her family, gave us strength; she also gave us *The New Ships,* and wrote in it: "The horses of hope run fast but the asses of experience amble thoughtfully." And Clover, now gone, our beautiful Maroon mountain hiker and friend.

Sasstree, friend, constant companion. Jah Son, backbone of the village. Perth, the pirate. Morris, the tailor. Mr. Denzel, water-bearer, fruit-bringer, savior in the worst of weathers. Vincent, the tam man. Michael Higgins, natural mystic. Selvin Johnson for the early Bob memories, and for the akete drumming. Georgie who made the fire light and told the little birdy story. Countryman who counseled on running, swimming, and being.

Everyone in Castle Gordon and Port Maria. All the students and teachers who came just to learn but left so much the richer in spirit.

INTRODUCTION

Rastafarians in Jamaica

The Children of Solomon

I began collecting the material for this book in 1985 when we made our first trip to Jamaica. The year 1985 in Jamaica, was just like the 1970s because that is how it works in what is called a third world country, an island nation, a world unto itself. It lives, as some might say, in the past. And the past is always very much present in the West Indies as island nations still struggle with neocolonial government and the conditions that Bob Marley called "mental slavery." But the book is not only about this.

This book is about people. A particular group of people who are as much misunderstood now as they were in the 1930s when they appeared on the scene with surprising vehemence, urging social and spiritual change in an indifferent and antithetical world. Perhaps it began with the St. Ann revolutionary Marcus Garvey who stated clearly what the Bible had already said: "Look to Africa, when a black King shall be crowned for the day of deliverance is near." He might very well have said that the king was Haile Selassie I of Ethiopia and that he was not only a king but a deity, descended from the House of David.

Singularly, the most important thing was that this king would bring forth a new day on earth. That his ancestral lineage included Jesus of Nazareth was perhaps less important than his direct familial connection to King Solomon, author of Ecclesiastes and considered by Rastafarians to be the wisest man who ever lived.

The children of Solomon are the children of Africans. And so it is said, as well, that "God come black." Haile Selassie was, according to Rastafarians we know, a black man and they ask: "Was not Jesus also black? And all of the Biblical Fathers of the Old Testament?"

These are the foundation of the conversations found in this book. The conversations themselves—spoken by country- and city-dwelling Rastafarians—revolve around issues that concern us today. How do I get bread to eat? How do I get money to live? Bob Marley, once again, turned this into a koan: "How do I work my more to get my less?"

This is still the conundrum in Jamaica, and now in many of the "first world" countries of the world including America, which has fast turned into a stratified nightmare of rich and poor, with an indecisive government that, like Jamaica in the 1980s, teeters between the extremes.

For more than ten summers, my wife and I ran a small Outward Bound type of school on the North Coast of Jamaica. During that time we traveled the parishes and visited every one, camped, bused, hiked, ran, swam, and climbed every accessible and inaccessible cranny of this beautiful, hardy, resilient island. In time, we would come to know Jamaica from the inside out, and time after time, we would reason with Rastafarians, listen to them talk about the birth of the world, their world, the world of Creation, the world of the moment we were in, the one just past, the one soon come, as they said.

We met men who had known Marcus Garvey, and who had heard Haile Selassie I speak. We listened to a man who said he was once Jonah riding in the belly of a whale. We heard tale tellers, ital chefs, men of reason, women of wisdom, but always we were included, not excluded, and during these years our eyes opened wide to a resourceful, spiritual way of life that is, sad to say, mostly gone in the Jamaica of today.

The conversations in this book seem a bit lost in time to us. They were recorded before some of the present-day Rastafarians, black and white, were born. Those who were alive were probably a little too young to listen to the scriptural poetry and storytelling of the past. Was it one minute ago that all this happened? It seems so to us. But at the same time, it also seems to have happened long ago.

Jamaica is a timeless country, an undiscovered country in a way. We have met only a few people who have followed in the literal footsteps of the revolutionary leader, Nanny, when she trekked from Moore Town to Accompong to meet with the great rebel leader Cujo. We did it while the sluices of rain came down off the limestone jungle cliffs, and the stories of Rastafarian friends poured down with them.

When you hear people speak in an ancient place, you will travel in time with them. Listen well to these elders, for who knows, while you hear their words you may be borne along with them and awaken, as we did, in another country, another time.

I

Heart

*My son, if thou wilt receive my words, and hide my
  commandments with thee;*
*So that thou incline thine ear unto wisdom, and apply
  thine heart to understanding;*
*Yea, if thou criest after knowledge, and liftest up thy voice
  for understanding;*
*If thou seekest her as silver, and searchest for her as hid
  treasures;*
*Then shalt thou understand the fear of the Lord, and find
  the knowledge of God.*
*For the Lord giveth wisdom: out of his mouth cometh
  knowledge and understanding.*
*He layeth up sound wisdom for the righteous: he is a
  buckler to them that walk uprightly.*
*He keepeth the paths of judgment and preserveth the way
  of his saints.*
*Then shalt thou understand righteousness, and judgment,
  and equity; yea, every good path.*

PROVERBS 2:1–9

The Jamaican brethren sit around a table late at night, drinking in the cool trade wind that was once known as the undertaker's breeze, since it combed the island only after dark. It is a great relief from the hot sun and from the work of the day. The gathering of Rastas, casual and unplanned, people coming and going in the yard, is the way of most evenings here in the small fishing village of Port Maria on the north coast of Jamaica.

People come and go, stopping for a short while to let go a few frustrations, tell a tale or two, laugh and smoke a spliff, sip a warm beer under the waning yellow moon. The voices, rhythmic as the rolling tide, speak about the day and their part in it. The people call this kind of easy conversation, this talking to one another with the heart: "reasoning." And they feel that the use of heartfelt words raises common, simple human beings to a state of beatitude, of divine redemption.

Tonight's reasoning session begins when someone asks a rhetorical question about life; about the things that are important to do in this life. Then, as often happens in a Rastafarian community, people seem to fall out of the night, both men and women, to, as they put it, "Link up thoughts, come together through the gentle art of reasoning." By and by, there is a large reasoning session, and the voices take on emotive hues. Some grow vexed and strident, others drop, low and wary. However, as the voices are raised and lowered, laughter spills out into the salty night sky, splashing at the feet of those who would argue to no purpose. Where there is laughter, there is no anger. The fire leaps up, finds no fuel, is put out with laughter.

I am listening, not really participating, just sitting and wondering how long this session will continue; I know, for instance, that it might go on all night. For each person is, in a sense, sending forth a devotional message. Yes, the session has turned, in its own way, prayerful. "This is what Jah give me," a man professes, "but this is what I need." He makes a kind of categorical list of things with which his life might move forward without obstruction. He is a fisherman, he needs a new boat; he needs to catch more fish. He is traveling ninety miles out to sea, touching the coast of Cuba to catch fish and sell them back in Port Maria. He needs a good boat with a strong outboard engine to carry him.

As I listen, I watch the moths, which are called "bats," in Jamaica.

They flutter about the open veranda. The small white owl, which people here still call "Patoo" after the gentle Arawak, alights in a Poinciana tree, then drops down without a sound to the bamboo fence that separates the enclosed yard from the road. Occasionally, a dog yelps, but the night noises are overruled by the dominant sounds of the sea.

It seems to me that the reasoning might not end at all, that it might go on for days. Someone is reciting, at the moment, a vast archive of personal needs. Then a man is saying, "If I just had a car that would run, and not break down all the time." And another says, "I have a car that runs, but no money for gas." Another, "I have no money, no car, but plenty of gas."

A young Rasta says, "I have all that I need to finish my house: zinc, windows, so it is just a matter of time before I get a door."

Now a woman, whose name is Clover, pushes in among the men to have her say: "I need medicine for my children," she says sharply. "None of this dibby-dibby stuff you all talk about. I need medicine for my mother, who is ailing. I need food for her two children. What is all this talk about material goods? I just want food and medicine."

A deep-voiced Rasta, Vincent, confides, "Darling, you don't look well."

"True," she says. "I have the jaundice, and need some medicine myself."

One man, sitting in the corner of the veranda, not saying anything, suddenly gets out of his wicker chair, and stretches his arms. He yawns. His name is Benji, and usually he has something to say, but apparently not this night. He begins to walk off, and Vincent calls to him. "You nuh seh nuttin', Benji." There is a soft questioning insistence in Vincent's voice.

Benji turns to face the group. He has what Jamaicans call "the permanent screw," a deeply wrinkled brow. He stands with his back to the sea, lean and angry, hungry looking. Benji scowls, his mouth tightly pursed. Once again, he starts to leave. He is wearing a pair of pants and no shirt. His dark muscled arms and powerful chest gleam in the dark. His eyes flash fire. He glances furiously around the veranda and says, "All this talk a lot of foolishness."

"Why?" I ask.

He seems reluctant to speak, as if something is tugging at him from the dark hill over the house; some secret magnetic attraction out there in the great-shouldered hillscape of night-darkened mango and pimento trees.

Everyone waits on his words.

"It a sin," he sighs, at last, "to ask for what you already have. You see," he adds softly, "Solomon was the wisest man, seen? But, if you check it out, you realize that even so great a man as Solomon, him beg for something he nuh have."

A silence has fallen over the group of brethren.

"And what was that?" I ask Benji.

"Him want a certain woman. Him want more children. Him nuh satisfy. No, mon. Not even Solomon, the wisest man on earth."

I add, "He had these things, but he still wanted them?"

"Ahh!" Benji shouts. "No man ever satisfy. That is why I seh talk foolish. Me nuh want nuttin' but what is given by Jah. And, for that, thanks and praises! For, what Jah give, no man tek way."

There is a murmuring of assent over the sea swell.

"What has Jah given you, Benji?" I question.

He laughs. His eyes gleam. He steps before me. "You don't know?"

I shake my head.

"Life, mon," Benji booms. "No thing more precious than life. Last winter me a go on a job, and me work a backhoe, and that machine flip over into a gully, and rip up me chest. Me almost die inna Kingston hospital. But me a go live. Me haffa live. Jah seh no, Benji, your time nuh come yet. So Benji live."

I look at his chest and in the pale light I can see the long scar that begins at the belt and ends just under his heart.

Benji turns to go, I follow him out. Everyone on the veranda is agreeing that what Benji says is true. Talk is foolishness.

At the gate, Benji says this to me: "The woman with the sick kids and the mother living with her, the one name Clover."

"Yes."

"She tough. Her a survivor."

"Yes," I agree.

"She gonna learn," Benji says sternly. "Jah gonna teach Clover a good likkle lesson."

I say nothing. For a moment we hear the night crickets, the tree frogs, the sea.

"Is the sufferers find God," Benji continues, going out the gate into the night. Then he adds, walking swiftly away, "Is the sufferers find peace."

"Like Job?" I call after him.

"Like Solomon," he answers.

I think about Solomon a lot. Was he the wisest man who ever lived, as all the local rootsmen say?

We have no one wiser today.

You might even say; we have no one wise today.

Not like ancient times anyway.

Solomon said to the Lord: "I am but a little child: I know not how to go out or come in" (1 Kings 3:7).

Solomon asked for one thing—"an understanding heart." This, God granted him. But, later, in his suffering over the love of an Egyptian woman who worshiped idols, God took away his understanding, and he was given instead his portion of suffering.

At last he attained beatitude, knowing, like David his father before him, that his son would achieve what he himself was unable to do. It was then his suffering ended, and so, too, his life, but not his wisdom: "Wherefore I perceive that there is nothing better, than that a man should rejoice in his own works; for that is his portion: for who shall bring him to see what shall be after him" (Ecclesiastes 3:22)?

It is Mackie, my closest friend, who tells me, "Heart is the wise one, not Solomon, and heart is in each one of us. To be Rasta you must have only this. Everyone talks about the colors red, gold, and green, but there is only red inside of you and me and without heart to run the red, we are not even alive."

2

Bird

For, lo, the winter is past, the rain is over and gone;
The flowers appear on the earth; the time of the singing of
birds is come, and the voice of the turtle dove is heard
in our land;
The fig tree putteth forth her green figs, and the vines
with the tender grape give a good smell. Arise, my
love, my fair one, and come away.
O my dove, that art in the clefts of the rock, in the secret
places of the stairs, let me see thy countenance, let
me hear thy voice; for sweet is thy voice, and thy
countenance is comely.

SONG OF SOLOMON 2:11–14

The Bible tells us in 1 Kings 4:32 that Solomon spoke 3,000 proverbs and 1,005 songs. Mythology informs that by means of a magic circlet—the legendary King Solomon's Ring—the great king conversed in the language of animals. He spoke easily to birds, beasts, and fishes. His wisdom came from the earth and his heart, and the words he spoke were silver and gold, so that the worldly and the lowly gave ear to what he said and quoted him as if his words had sprung from their own lips. As the English writer Rudyard Kipling described in the poem "There Was Never a Queen Like Balkis,"

There never was a king like Solomon
Not since the world began
Yet Solomon talked to a butterfly
As a man would talk to a man.

There is an Arabic myth wherein Solomon summons the Queen of Sheba by speaking to a little bird, and in this same story Solomon is said to travel upon the air on a magic carpet of green silk. Overhead, an armada of birds flew above him to shield him from the sun. One day, however, one of the birds told Solomon that she had been far to the south. There, she said, it was her pleasure to view a great queen, whose people worshipped the sun.

Solomon learned from his advisors that the bird was right. And he soon learned that the queen whose kingdom he had heard about was none other than the Queen of Sheba.

Therefore he summoned the little bird and gave her a letter perfumed with musk and sealed by himself with the royal seal.

And the messenger flew off to deliver the letter. Upon reaching Queen Makeda's (Queen of Sheba's) courtyard, the bird dropped the letter on her lap, and returned to the king. (The theme of the little bird delivering "songs pure and true" is mentioned in the song "Three Little Birds" by Bob Marley.)

When we first came to stay near Port Maria, Jamaica, there was a tuck shop that sold cassettes, and it was named "Three Little Birds." Bob Marley's wife, Rita, owned the shop. We used to pass the time of day in that little music store reasoning with a friend of Bob's from the '70s, a Rasta named Selvin Johnson.

Selvin's voice was whispery, and when he spoke softly and mysteriously he almost sounded like a little warbler. Selvin once told me about the Jamaican doctorbird, the largest swallow-tailed hummingbird in the world. Not long after he describes them I see one dipping around the blossoms of a flame heart tree.

Selvin tells me that the Arawak Indians, the first inhabitants of Jamaica, believe that doctorbirds are messengers from the spirit world. If you could have seen their tails scissoring in the sun, their invisible wings blurring the air, you would not doubt Selvin's love of this angelic bird.

One day Selvin takes us up the hill to Bob Marley's old house in St. Mary. We wander in the deep shade of the pimento trees while high above our heads lying on long gray limbs, tree-dwelling iguanas sprawl in the stillness, with only their gold eye moving in the green.

Bob's house seems abandoned, but inside there are the scattered school books of Ziggy and Steve Marley, journals they had kept in pencil; but I don't look at them, and we walk out back with Selvin. He tells me Bob had a brand-new Mercedes here once and that it cost twice the price of the car to have it shipped to Jamaica. "Bob drove it only once around the driveway," Selvin says sadly.

"What happened after that?"

"Him die of a cancer."

"Yes, I know about that."

"But him no die," Selvin says.

"You mean, in the physical sense," I add.

"The structure gone, but the foundation strong, and stay firm like Solomon. The words them. The words him say. One day them mek a Bible fe we."

The following day we journey to Kingston to visit Bob's main residence, which is now the Bob Marley Museum, at 56 Hope Road. The bullet holes from the attempted assassination of Bob, Rita, and others are still there, reminding us of that awful night in November 1976, when unnamed gunmen forced their way into the house and began to blast away at all who were present. When they left, Bob Marley, Rita Marley, and Bob's manager, Don Taylor, were all struck, but none killed. The murderous days of the Kingston ghetto wars and political uprisings still hang over the house.

I put my finger in one of those holes, and sense something of a jolt, as if my index finger were being inserted into an orifice of history. How deep it is and how strange to feel the legend of that awful night come alive in this hole in the wall.

The house where the poet of reggae once reasoned with brethren from around the world has a curious emptiness about it. Some say he was the incarnation of King Solomon in our own troubled time. He tried certainly to bring together the disparate nations of war and exile, the frustrated legions of black and white in their separate camps of futile enmity.

Bob Marley once said, "Me no talk fe no white and me no talk fe no black. Me just talk fe the Creator and fe that vibration that we must all come together and live." And whatever he said was heard. Much of it was written down. Indeed some of it does sound like it has sprung from the Bible, or from the world-weary mouth of wise Solomon, or from an all-knowing little bird, a doctorbird, perhaps.

Walking in the yard where Bob's reasoning sessions stretched across the indigo nights and into the bright dawns of sad tomorrows, I hear in my mind the things he said. Solomon, they say, Solomon: Words from the heart and the earth. Words from the soul of man.

Bob once said, "I am one of the Twelve Tribes of Israel . . . the twelve sons of Israel, representing the twelve tendencies of man from Reuben to Benjamin so that every man is born in one of the twelve months and each month is represented by a tribe. So like for me, come from the Tribe of Joseph, and Haile Selassie, the Conquering Lion, is of the Tribe of Judah."

Out in the yard we find an old Rastaman cooking porridge over a logwood fire. The thick yellowy cornmeal bubbles in the well-used, blackened pot. We join him, and I, sensing something special about him, sit down and ask what it was like when Bob was here.

He tells me that his name is Georgie.

So *this* is Georgie, the mystic logwood lighter and porridge maker. The man who fed and warmed the hard-hearted and the faint of heart, the man who made the light come out of darkness, and when the football players in Bob's youth showed up, cold, tired, hungry, this man, this Georgie, this half-mad tender of fires, gave the firelight warmth, the cornmeal porridge that Bob celebrated in one of his greatest songs, "No Woman, No Cry."

A banana quit flits across the yard, whispering *sssssss* as it darts from tree to tree.

Georgie stops stirring his porridge, looks into my face, and starts to tell of a little bird that once flew away far across the heavens.

He was on a ship at sea, he told me, when suddenly this little bird messenger of heaven lit on his head and rested there for a moment. "The ship rocks," Georgie said, "and the bird's feet tangle in my locks." Remembering this, he burst out laughing.

Then, he said, poetically, the bird dissolved into the eventide and the empty ocean spaces.

"Dissolved?" I ask.

"Him turn fool'n fly," he says, face cracking into a wild smile.

Georgie turns to the fire. He picks up a piece of logwood, splits it in two with his machete. "You know what happen that likkle bird?" Georgie asks.

"What?"

"Him get a re-charge offa me head. And that carry him to land."

I nod, visualizing it.

"Y'understand wha me say?" His eyes pierce into mine.

"You . . . grounded him, gave him earth . . . for one brief little second."

"Just so. Him kotch up inna me hair, an him feel de land vibe, cause me a-come fresh from de land, and de land still inna me bone, an brain, an hair."

"What did the little bird give to *you*?" I ask Georgie.

"Well . . ." He hacks, spits, coughs. Touches his temple with a forefinger. Whispering, Georgie says, "Bird gi me wisdom. Me feel im still. Him vibe sweet, mon. Sweet like the breath of Jah."

We share some porridge, Georgie and me. No one seems to notice us standing in the jamdown uptown heat, tasting cornmeal porridge at 56 Hope Road.

Georgie was around when things heated up in the '70s when burning and looting swept the Kingston streets. Babylon world going down. Sodom and Gomorrah, pillar of salt, endtimes. The graffiti of neocolonial failure written on Gun Court prison walls and etched in the faces of elders like Georgie who had seen the best minds of his generation destroyed by poverty, oppression, injustice, and madness: he himself no exception to the rule although he doesn't know he's crazy. Rather he thinks the world is crazy and he is sane. And in some quixotic, wild mystic sense, he is right.

Eating porridge, sitting on a round stone, I ask him, "You think that little bird will come back?"

Georgie pokes the fire with a firestick. "So it written, for, as the man did say, 'Been 'ere before, come back again.'"

3

Iron

And when Jesus came into the ruler's house, and saw
the minstrels and the people making a noise, he said
unto them, "Give place: for the maid is not dead, but
sleepeth."
And they laughed him to scorn.
But when the people were put forth, he went in, and took
her by the hand and the maid arose.
And the fame hereof went abroad and to all that land.
And when Jesus departed thence, two blind men followed
him, crying, and saying, "Thou Son of David, have
mercy on us."
And when he was come into the house the blindmen came
to him: and Jesus saith unto them, "Believe ye that I
am able to do this?" They said unto him, "Yea, Lord."
Then touched he their eyes, saying, "According to your
faith be it unto you."
And their eyes were opened; and Jesus straightly charged
them, saying, "See that no man know it."

MATTHEW 9:23–30

The thing that most impressed Queen Makeda about King Solomon was his cool manner, his calm. Then, too, the words of his mouth were treasure showing that he was truly one with the Father.

How did this son of David come to be so wise?

There are answers to this in the Kebra Nagast, which means the "Glory of the Kings" in Amharic. My friend Mackie calls this holy book "an African version of the Bible ripped out of the King James version." When I asked him who did this, he answered, "The scribes of King James."

"Why did they excise it?"

Mackie said, "Like them say, 'God come black.' The scribes them don't like that, so it have to go." Some people here say that Solomon's faith was his greatest virtue. They say that faith alone provided him with gladness of heart, and that Ecclesiastes is full of that, as well as the sorrow of life under the sun. But it was Solomon's silver tongue that gave him glory, passion in the living, heartfulness in the speaking; the lack of which Solomon said himself causes such grief: the fall of nations comes from it.

The corruption of spirit in the kingdoms of the world—both great and small—comes from the rulers of the lands not having tribute of heart; this you hear from many old school Rastas, especially the ones who live hidden away in the hills. "Heart," they say, "reigns where love is." Heart, spirit, vibes. Word, sound, power. Without these, there is nothing. The world is nothing without them.

Solomon, being the wisest man, knew this. So the country Rastas, the regional rootsmen of St. Mary and St. Ann, say to me when I talk to them. They quote Solomon as if he were there with them, nodding with tacit approval.

"To know Jah," Solomon says, "is to see with the eyes of the newborn." On the lips of the Rastas, you hear such quotes. Just the other day I listened to a fisherman, "a fisher of men," as he said of himself:

"What is the use of us, the children of men, if we do not live by kindness, if we do not exhibit love in our actions? Are we not nothingness, mere grass of the field, which dries up in its season, and is devoured by flame from heaven when we do not rise up and show our humanity and become men of wisdom?"

In Jamaica today there are those who believe that Solomon is alive and well, moving among the people in the market, hammering nails on the builder's scaffold, throwing mended net into the fisherman's boat, *speechifying,* as they would have it, shaping words as the harpists of old plucked tunes from the incendiary air and drummed by firelight under the numberless stars.

Peter Tosh, reggae singer, songwriter, founding member of the Wailers, once said:

"Remember Moses, remember Moses? That man no dead; that man trod the earth still."

And so it is with Solomon.

These days in Jamaica it takes the wisdom of Solomon and the courage of Moses just to stay alive. The dollar, *Sammy dollar* Tosh called it, is slipping away.

"I never thought, as a child, I would see people disrespect a money," our friend Roy McKay says one day, "but look, now, coin is useless, Babylon money, worthless. Shilling and pence days was more better, at least dem money had value [eighty-nine to one U.S. dollar at the present time]. Every day it costs more to live; every day prices higher, money lower."

Yet Solomonic faith seems to be Jah's great gift to Jamaica. In abundance, in perpetuity, in everything people do or say, it is faith. Remembrance of the past, all the way back to slave days, as they say, doesn't cancel faith in the future. This is paradoxical, bewildering to some, but true for many.

Roy continues, "I have lived to see the farmer's prophecy fulfilled: better to have a tree that yields ackee than an account at the bank that yields grief. Bob was a farmer, y'know. Whenever him tek a break, him farm, him till the soil as him did as a child wid him grandfather Omeriah."

Roy is right, these days a tin of milk, a loaf of bread, even a chicken back is costly. There is hunger in the land, and Bob Marley's words, like Solomon's, are full of truth: "A hungry man is an angry man." For the rich it might be no more than a mere annoyance, the collapse of the post-colonial economy, but to the poor it's no less than murder in the street.

You don't see street anger here in the fishing village of Port Maria on the North Coast of Jamaica. You see thinly worn clothes and worn-thin tempers. You see poverty but the country people's eyes shine with hope still, and at night while walking along an unlit street with the tree frogs chiming, people pass in the darkness, people whom we cannot see but who always have a kind word of greeting. The darkness becomes light when you meet someone on a community path. When a Rastaman passes on the road, he says, "Yes-I," meaning, you-and-I know one another, we are each what we are but we are one. We are positive people.

Some say, "Respect."

Some say, "Guidance."

Some say, "Positive."

Such words, spoken from the heart, proclaim that all is well, that things are good no matter what the devils do, no matter what the draculizers, the money-mongers, the Babylon do. Words of greeting like *positive* and *guidance* are a reminder that with a watchful eye one is well protected at all times. In the time of darkness, one can see.

One of my favorite Rasta friends, one that I've not mentioned yet, is a man with laughing eyes named "Irons." The name comes from his carbon-forged, righteous spirit, and his seeing into things, cutting through matter into the spiritual essence of life.

Irons spends much time sitting on a driftwood log near the compound where we live. He constructs wicker crafts, which he sells, wherever and whenever he can. When Irons is not at his wicker work, he is at sea, fishing. He is known as a fisherman, but like others, he's also a fisher of men.

Irons is shy and, though quite expressive, you must know him well before he will speak to you; and even then it is difficult to get Irons to talk. When he does his words are chosen and few. Mostly, he sits and smiles at some small secret meditation while his fingers are nimbly plaiting the wicker vines that make a curious whispery noise as he works in what would otherwise be total silence.

Normally, whenever Irons sees me he says, "Positive," in a voice that sounds like old sandpaper on sea-washed driftwood. One day I am sitting next to him under the broad-leaved almond trees, and I ask him what is meant by the word "positive." In other words, the religious—if there is one—meaning. He smiles showing his straight white teeth. His eyes, with their slight almond uplift and down-turn at the corner by the bridge of his nose, are always bright and merry. I enjoy looking at him, and I am hardly unique in this, for Irons has a glow about him that everyone seems to like and to share. He has many friends and no enemies.

How I would love to tap into his unique faith to find the secret wellspring from which it originates. For there is no one hereabouts who expresses such a Solomonic gladness about being alive; who asks for little and who remains so true to his name that I frequently think of the Solomonic proverb, "Iron sharpeneth iron." But what spiritual iron, exactly, does Irons use as his heart-to-heart foil?

Someone who should know better tells me: "Irons has no problems, that he just leads an 'Irie life.'" I know better. Although he may lead a simple life of contemplation and compassion, Irons, like all the rest of us, has his problems, no doubt. However, he must, as evidenced by his manner—and I have known him more than thirteen years—remain on his rock. He seems peaceful, no matter what.

Problems, though, most of us would agree, are the natural province of humankind: the inheritance of human nature. Or are they? Irons, by his presence alone, denies that. If he has trials and tribulations, no one, not even his closest friends, knows about them.

Sitting in silence next to Irons, watching his fingers do the wicker dance, I remember a crazed person that I saw in Ocho Rios only a few hours earlier. The man had come up to me, shifty-eyed and nervous:

the antithesis of Irons and his implacable calm. I watched him make a quick little mime of thumb and forefinger, the cocaine seller's silent routine. I shake him off, but now he comes back with a new twist: he flexes his fingers again, turning index and second finger into the spliff mandala. (If you don't want a sniff, do you want a smoke?) Once again, I shake my head, no. So the squirrely-eyed one says out loud, in frustration, "You want mushroom? Pills? Uppers, downers, between-ers? What?"

I laugh. "I have enough problems without that," I tell him. He eyes me suspiciously. Then tosses over his shoulder, "You don't know what problems is," and disappears into the throng of this self-conscious little Babylon city.

Of course, coming from America, and having American dollars to spend here in Jamaica, entitles him to be correct about this assumption. And, if I have no problems to speak of, as the man says, why am I seeking the solace of someone like Irons? Perhaps being around Irons, and those like him, spending time with Rastas whose refusal to buy into contemporary culture, is so refreshing to me, that it becomes—has become—a kind of luminary fix, for which I am constantly grateful.

But Irons, now, I wonder: does he know what problems are?

I am curious to know of his inner life. He is more than a little mysterious, aloof, otherworldly.

"Irons, how is it that you can sit all day and not sell anything—and still not care?" His quick fingers stop flickering for a moment.

"I care."

"But you don't get vexed."

"No, I don't vex."

"If you don't sell, you don't eat—right?"

"If I don't sell, I don't sell."

He smiles, this amuses him. He starts to laugh. It is an infectious laugh, a faint peeling of distant bells, a singing like water spilling.

"I have problems," he says, "just like everybody else."

But that is all he says, and he goes back to work, his fingers flying, the wicker lashing, side to side, winnowing the air.

I try and draw him out a bit further.

"You don't push your works on people, like they do in Ochy. On the other hand, you don't make the sales they make there."

He smiles. "That is true."

Back to the wicker, the strong fingers plaiting the pliant threads of brown vine. When he is done, the hat he is making will be able to hold water. The weave will be that tight. No one works that well in wicker any more. Irons must have learned this trade from an elder, who, in turn, learned it from another. For all we know, this ancient art is sold in the bazaars of Western Africa today. It is a very old African thing, wicker-work, and nothing lasts longer or is more durable in a tropical climate. Wicker lives forever, if treated with care.

"Irons, where do you get your peace of mind?"

This really cracks him up—as it was meant to—the overt approach. Ask and you shall receive.

A full minute goes by while Irons smiles to himself. His fingers, like miniature wrestlers, throw the wickers off balance and thread them through.

"Positive vibrations," he says, at last.

"From what?"

"Jah."

I figured all along that our conversation might end at such a juncture—for, if you have what Irons has within him—it is pretty much impossible to explain how it got there. But, for the record, I had to ask, and I did, and that is that.

However, just as I am about to leave him, Irons asks, "Do you wish to have the same faith that I do?"

"I would like to know where it comes from."

"Very well. Tomorrow, I will bring you 'The Book.'"

I have a deep suspicion that this book might be one of three things: *The Book of Enoch,* an Ethiopian version of one of the lost volumes of the Bible; the Maccabee Bible, which was outlawed in Jamaica since before the time of Emancipation in 1834; or perhaps the Kebra Nagast.

Irons says good-bye, his sage-eyes crinkling, a smile on his lips. "I will bring The Book tomorrow," he affirms.

For the rest of that day, and a good part of that night, I am mesmerized by the thought of *The Book*. Possibly, it is not one of the texts I imagine it to be. Perhaps it is something far more esoteric.

Early next morning, after a restless sleep, I search out Irons. However, he is not sitting on his bark-stripped log. The haphazard rolls of wicker are not there either. And no one that I meet in the yard has seen him.

A week goes by. Irons does not seem to be anywhere. It seems he has vanished. I figure he is fishing. Still, I am a bit impatient to see The Book. Then, after a few more days of waiting, a friend tells me that Irons has gone to sea. He is fishing for some big fish, his friend says. The sea is lying flat, as they say, and Irons, being a fisherman, is taking advantage of the calm. "Don't worry you will see him again," the lady-friend says. "He is here all the while with his wickers."

Several weeks pass. No Irons. Then, one morning when I am not expecting to see him, he is there, just like always, smiling, his fingers dancing. "Irons," I say, in surprise, "I missed you."

"I was at sea." He laughs. Then, "You know, first it was flat, the water calm. Then there was a storm, and we lost our traps. Then the boat sprung a leak. Then it sank. And we had to swim for shore. This took us a long time, a day, or more."

"You're kidding."

He is perfectly serious.

"I haven't seen you for weeks."

"Then my friend, who owned the boat, got sick and I had to take care of his family for him."

Irons grins, "I am lucky to be alive."

"I need a hat," I tell him. "No, a few hats."

He looks at me blankly, then his eyes crinkle.

"I shouldn't have gone to sea," he remarks. "I should've stayed here and made you some hats."

"Maybe I wouldn't have needed them then," I say facetiously.

Irons chuckles over this. Then he adds, almost inaudibly, "Did you like The Book?" He is staring at the hat he is making, rounding out the brim.

"What book?"

He puts the hat on his knees.

"Didn't my lady-friend give it to you?"

"No. She just said you'd soon be back."

"I asked her to put it in the kitchen for you."

"Maybe she did."

I get up and walk to the back of the yard and go into the kitchen. There is a coverless book, very beaten up, lying by the telephone. I examine it and see the cover has fallen off; the pages are yellowed and torn, and turned, by sea and moisture, to the ghostly consistency of toilet paper. The binding is intact, but the pages are leaves about to fall off the tree. I turn a page or two and come to the title page: *The Power of Positive Thinking* by Dr. Norman Vincent Peale.

Back at the wicker-site, I try to hide my obvious disappointment. This venerable old bestseller used to sit on my mother's night table when I was growing up. She read it many times, and she tried to get me to read it but being rebellious I refused.

How curious it is that the things we turn away from have a way of coming back to haunt us.

So now my mother's cherished classic, the same book I had spent a lifetime evading was returned to me by a rootsman I greatly admired.

Was he joking? No, Rastas don't make ironic jokes; they don't even perceive irony, for, in truth, what is irony other than the twisted appearance of good news turned bad? Clearly, Irons was offering me something that he cherished. I could see that in his beatific expression. But, to me, it was a bit ironic. Maybe more than a bit.

"The Book has everything you will ever need," Irons states matter-of-factly.

I stand before him flipping pages appearing to be reading, but really, I am wondering how my mom's lesson plan had circled back, traveled thousands of sea miles to meet me on the north coast of Jamaica.

"If you don't have time to read it, it is all right," Irons says swiftly.

I continue to flip pages. What am I looking for?

"You don't have to read it at all," Irons tells me.

"I'm pretty busy right now," I answer lamely. The book has my mother's odd faith-healing written all over it, and I can even see her marginal notes in soft pencil calligraphy.

Then Irons says something I will always remember.

"There is a line in The Book that I have based my life on."

"What is it?"

"According to your faith be it unto you."

"That is from the New Testament, and Jesus said it."

Irons seems not to care where it came from, but he gently reminds me that he found it first in The Book.

"Do you pray a lot, Irons?"

Smiling, he admits, "What you think you see is a man doing wicker, what you should see is a man praying. And when I am at sea, fishing, that is also my prayer. And when I am asleep, dreaming, then I am praying still. Whatever I do, it is prayer. I learned that from The Book."

"But you're a Rasta."

"Does it make a difference?"

"I don't know . . . does it?"

Irons laughs. "Rasta takes any and all from each and all. Some Rasta prays in church. Other prays in the bush. What matter where you pray? Or where you find knowledge so long as you do find it? We should grow wise like Solomon, for that is natural to any but a fool. But remember that Solomon the man said: 'Be innocent as a dove, wise as a serpent.'"

"True."

The Book flutters in my hands in the sea wind. It makes a quiet flutter like bird's wings.

"You see," Irons says, "it is alive."

Mackie comes along and, hearing us reasoning, adds some thoughts of his own. "Every man is himself. Many are called and few are chosen, but I say that I can be one of the chosen, if I just be myself. Therefore, I am a free man. That is what I declare. And if the church had a devotion,

I could be there. And if the obeah man had a devotion, I could be there. And if the Rastaman had a devotion, I could be there. Do you see? A free man can choose where him want to be. Bob said it like this: 'Some are the roots and some are the branches.' But I say, as Solomon, leave the judgment to the Father. Believe what you want to believe, but remain open, free."

"Is that what it means to be Rasta?" I ask.

"I cannot speak for any but I," Mackie says.

Irons keeps working, smiling. Working, smiling.

Mackie continues. "'If you know what life is really worth,' Bob said, 'you would get yours on earth.' That mean, everything just go on and on, the tree has to grow, has to die. Since ancient days people been killing, stealing; and today, killing, stealing just the same. Even in the Bible, the great Isaac, the great Joseph, died. Every man dies individually. But as Bob did say, 'if there is a Father to come on judgment day, then that day is every day; each and every day that we are alive. And after that, no one knows. But life, we know, goes on. Life must go on.' And as Bob say, too, 'The half has never been told.' So, you see, what it means to be a man; and a Rastaman is a man. So it is just like that these days—each day—judgment day."

While Mackie is speaking, he is moving, which is why his town name, secret name, is "cock-a-roach."

Irons is bent, head down, spider hands working like Anansi, the African prince, weaving webs no man can get out of, which is, perhaps why he keeps that smile affixed to his lips, why he is ever on the verge of laughing.

After a while, when no one speaks—when Mackie looks out to the harbor where the sea cracks white on the reef—Irons starts to laugh.

It starts quietly, softly. But the laughter is steady like the sea, and grows in volume. Finally, Irons looks at Mackie and says, "True, Mackie. You speak the truth."

"I was saying," Mackie adds, his voice a low rumble, "that this book you are holding, or any book anyone is holding, then so be it. For the word is everywhere, and in everything, and the word is the Word."

Irons looks up, face in repose, serious.

"True, Mackie."

"What I am saying dem did say long time past." Mackie says, phrasing the patois just so, and so deeply you almost can't hear him over the sea roar.

The book in my lap casts a glow. It is an old, tattered, mildewed, sea-warped, ruined assemblage of worm-eaten, cockroach-trodden pages so soft they feel like ancient cotton to my fingers.

"I promise you, Irons, I will read it."

Irons nods solemnly but mostly to himself.

Time passes. Time and the summer slip away.

Fall comes, and the cooler weather arrives in Jamaica.

I can't explain exactly why, except for the image of my mom's calligraphy, but I do not find the time to read the book. I don't read much of anything. I listen. I hardly talk. I just listen. The Book sits on a night-stand by the bed. And when I go to bed at night, I remember all the conversations of the day and the words come and go in my head, and I write them down as I hear them.

But The Book now sits on my night table, unread.

And sometimes the pages flutter in the sea breeze late at night, and a sense of guilt overcomes me. But still I write on . . . .

I see Irons from time to time. He does not mention The Book.

I don't speak of it to him either. We go our ways, tending to our lives.

One day I am in town, wandering around the old stone Anglican church. I like the cemetery by the sea, the sixteenth-century graves against the blue of the sea.

This day I am surprised by a well-dressed woman lying down at the head of a stone marker. She is lying flat on her back, looking up at the sky, and at first, I think she has fallen ill. I bend down.

"Are you all right?" I ask.

The woman's eyes flutter open. She looks at me as if I were a Jamaican ghost, a "duppy." "I come here often to visit my husband," she explains. She doesn't move. Her arms lie at her side.

"Where is he?"

"Right under me," she replies. Then goes on, "One day, soon, I join my beloved. But I don't go join him in the earth, not me. I don't bury in the sand like this."

"And why not?" I ask, hoping to get more story out of her.

The woman is a sight, lying there in her best clothes, flat on her back, not minding the sun in her eyes. She talks to me as if we did this every day: a little graveyard chatty-chatty sort of thing.

"I want to swim alone," she tells me.

"Swim?' I scratch my head. "You mean you want to be buried at sea?"

"No, mon," she chides. "I want to swim through the sky up to God. I want to fly home, you see. But the way I see it—it like floating in the current of the Lord."

"You say it so beautifully."

I walk back to the house thinking of what the woman said to me. Is this the answer to our prayers? That we should see the parting in the weave, where the threads are not yet interlocked? Where the lines of linear thought are missing, gone? Where odd and even are the same? The everwhere. The blue on blue of eternal grace, beatification. The dream of time, of times, of lost time in Babylon. The Arawak word *coyaba* comes to mind. The word means "heaven." The real thing. The real place. It seems, it seemed, so real coming out of her mouth, but even now as I walk I feel it slipping away. I feel it fading.

Back at our yard, Irons is there.

I see him, sitting on his log, smiling.

Weaving his wicker-withes.

Plaiting over, under, over, *swishhhh*.

Irons sees me.

He asks, "Have you read The Book?"

"I'm going to, right now."

For the rest of the day, I am reading Norman Vincent Peale's *The Power of Positive Thinking* while the sea breeze plays with the sun-faded pages, and the banana quits and the pocket parrots converse in the almond trees, and the sea has its say.

By sundown, I am finished.

I close the book, step out onto the veranda and look down.

Irons is there, weaving.

Or should I say, praying?

He looks up just as I look down.

Our eyes lock for a second.

He smiles, I smile.

I do not need to tell him I have read the book.

He knows.

Yet I have come to this conclusion: there is nothing, in Peale's thinking, that *is* or *is not,* Rastafarian.

The book is a serene smile, the kind that Irons makes when he is weaving. When he sees you seeing him, and all is well.

Yet all the words in Peale's journey of wisdom come to the same thing, come to less than the old woman lying down by her buried husband beside the soughing sea. All the great books, writ or unwrit, intact or tattered, are bested by a small, graveyard voice, singing to the surf that flies up like lace in the fine blue air: "One day I will swim up to God."

4

Fire

> *His eyes were as a flame of fire, and on his head were*
> *many crowns; and he had a name written that no*
> *man knew, but he himself.*
> *And he was clothed in a vesture dipped in blood: and his*
> *name is called The Word of God.*
> *And the armies, which were in heaven, followed him upon*
> *white horses, clothed in fine linen, white and clean.*
> *And out of his mouth goeth a sharp sword that with it he*
> *should smite the nations: and he shall rule them with*
> *a rod of iron: and he treadeth the winepress of the*
> *fierceness and wrath of Almighty God.*
> *And he hath on his vesture and on his thigh a name*
> *written, KING OF KINGS AND LORD OF*
> *LORDS.*
>
> REVELATION 19:12–16

Fire, the resolute Rastaman, who was once a Rasta preacher, a very rare career, is pacing in front of the sea. We are in the town of Annotto Bay. The blue sea, blinding white on the beach, crashes accompaniment to Fire's explosions of Rastafarian rage.

"There is only one Bible," he announces in his rich baritone voice. "I am not referring to the Ethiopian Bible, or the Christian Bible, but this Bible right here." He touches his heart. This gesture of gentleness is juxtaposed against his posture, pacing and tossing his locks, which, straight and beautifully groomed, hang down to his ankles—yes, his ankles—and they are a perfect curtain surrounding his head, shoulders, and the back of his body.

"I am saying," he continues, backed by the folding of the waves, "that it doesn't matter what book you read. What matters is how you live. If you live an honorable and righteous life, you are living the Bible, not just reading it."

Fire struts back and forth, his locks swinging in perfect time with the cymbals of the sea.

"Too many Rastas these days are accepting a lower standard of life, seeking out blood money and white women. These men are not even Rasta, for they have the wrong intention. These are the false prophets, the wolves in sheep's clothing."

I ask Fire if he thinks the movement—if it can be called that—has lost ground, if, in some way, it is faltering. His reply is emphatic.

"Listen," he says, "the reason I move so, as you see me, is that I used to be a preacher, well, a kind of Rastaman-reasoning-preacher man. I would go about wherever people wanted to hear the words of reasoning, and I would reason with them, just as you see me here now. They would ask a question, and I would answer them. Giving fire for fire."

He chuckles, whirls about, his locks whirling with him, black locks against the white locks of the sea.

"You see me now," he says rhetorically. "What do you see? Blackman? No. African? No. What, then?"

He waits, but he does not want me to answer. He merely wants me to think.

Suddenly Fire shouts at me: "I am an Ethiopian." He scowls now, challenging anyone—even the sea—to say that he is not an Ethiopian. The cadence of his voice comes and goes, lifting and dropping, with the assault of the waves on the beach, the two in concert, playing together. Forward and backward. Coming and going. Charge, retreat. Forward, backward. It is dizzying, this motion of Fire's by the soughing sea, the oratory sea. But it is also very beautiful, orchestrated this way; I have never seen or heard anything quite like it. The preacher and nature preaching together.

Then Fire lets out a long sigh.

"I don't preach anymore," he says so gently I can barely hear him.

"Why not?" I ask. "Are the younger Rastas not with you?"

Fire rubs his chin and looks out to sea.

"Most of these fellows," he remarks, "smoke a lot of herb."

He sighs again.

"I hardly smoke anymore." He grins and shakes his head.

"You just stopped?"

"Sometimes I boil the tea, but usually I don't partake of it. Look, I am with the Most High at all times. Why do I need ganja?"

"So you don't feel that the herb is the healing of the nations?"

The gleam in Fire's eye returns. "Reasoning, man to man, *that* is the healing of the nations, not herb."

"Just reasoning?"

"I believe in the power of Nyabinghi. As it ought to be translated: 'Death to white *and* black oppressors.' That is the true translation. Not, as some think, 'Death to *white* oppressors.' No, mon. You see, so many of my so-called brethren are holding the rest of us back. They see the color thing, nothing else. They want the white people down and the black people up. They don't understand that it isn't about people up or down. Through the power of the Most High, we should reason together. That way, we solve all of our problems. Yes, reasoning. The healing of the nations is sweet talk, angry talk, swift and ready talk, plain talk, talk among brothers and sisters, face to face, eye to eye, with nothing standing between."

Fire throws back his head. He laughs in the sun. His long locks lie upon his shoulders like a Galilean robe. Suddenly, he strides over to where I am sitting and offers me his fist. This is the old Jamaican greeting, not the various new ones. Our fists bump against one another roughly, warmly, knuckle to knuckle, real old-time Rasta style.

"Yes, reasoning . . ." he says. Then, "The herb brought us part of the way; we must go the rest of the way by ourselves. Just us. Reasoning will do it, talking among one another instead of feuding and fighting all the time. Not trying to pull one another down. But being together, peace and love. It really can work. It's that simple."

I say, "Until the color of a man's skin is no more significant than the color of his eyes."

Fire's fist touches mine.

He says, smiling in the sun, "It's not about the length of a man's locks. It's about being together, seeing the truth, the indivisible truth."

"Of reasoning," I add, and the knuckles are there again, two fists ratcheted together as one. And I feel the fire travel through us, so that both of us feel it deep within.

5

l and l

Is any among you afflicted? Let him pray. Is any merry?
    Let him sing psalms.
Is any sick among you? Let him call for the elders of the
    church; and let him pray over him, anointing him
    with oil in the name of the Lord.
And the prayer of faith shall save the sick, and the Lord
    shall raise him up; and if he has committed sins, they
    shall be forgiven him.
Confess your faults one to another, and pray for one
    another, that ye may be healed. The effectual fervent
    prayer of a righteous man availeth much.

JAMES 5:13–16

Go to now, ye that say, "Today or tomorrow we will go
    into such a city, and continue there a year, and buy
    and sell, and get gain."
Whereas ye know not what shall be on the morrow. For
    what is your life? It is even a vapor that appeareth for
    a little time and then vanisheth away.

> *For that ye ought to say, If the Lord will, we shall live,*
> *and do this, or that.*
> *But now ye rejoice in your boastings: all such rejoicing is*
> *evil. Therefore to him that knoweth to do good, and*
> *doeth it not, to him it is a sin.*
>
> JAMES 4:13–17

I am at a north coast reggae party, a veranda full of dancing and talking, but very little reasoning, and in that way it reminds me of an American party.

Bored with the noise, I join some Rastas on the back stairs of the rambling two-story colonial house. These guys must be feeling the way I do because they are tapping akete drums and softly chanting a duppy-chasing song.

"What ghosts are you trying to get rid of?" I ask.

"Those that are ruining this party," a drummer replies.

"Where do they come from?"

"From this place," a second drummer explains. He points to the earth. "They live here."

"And drumming gets rid of them?"

They each nod their heads but the dread sitting closest to me on the stairs adds, "Duppy don't abide two thing: drum and smoke."

"I see no smoke," I tell him.

"Get some," he says, laughing.

The other drummer, raising his hands high and coming down hard on the drum's goatskin rim, cries out, "Righteousness smoke."

The other shouts: "Light'ning and tunder!"

There is laughter, the ring and ping of akete. The high, tight-skinned, wonderful, ear-awakening, bell-ringing spell of tenor hand drums.

It is like a hard rain, these two drums; rain tripping on a galvan roof.

I move to one side of the drummers, and there is my old friend, Spreeboy, the gray-eyed Rasta elder. He waves a greeting to me and then, as if it were no trouble at all, begins to ascend a sixty-foot Jamaica

Tall coconut tree. Spreeboy is maybe eighty years of age, but an ageless climber of trees.

Up he goes, hopping with his feet, which are loosely bound with some tied-dried banana leaves. His hands pull up while his legs do a kind of hop up the high backbone of the curvatured, sea-arced tree that bends high over a canyon of purple croton bushes.

Spreeboy makes it to the top. Under a canopy of fronds, he disappears. And then comes the thunder of coconuts. They come down like hard green cannonballs, striking the earth with a mean thud, and rolling away under the croton and aurelia hedges.

After a little while, Spreeboy descends, gathers the coconuts into a crocus sack, hauls them to the back porch where the drummers and I await him. I've not seen Spreeboy for a while. His sprung dreadlocks seem to stick right straight out of his skull like sticks. He offers each of us a jelly, as they are called, and the four of us drink our fill of the clear water. After which we eat the jelly—the white, cool pudding inside the coconut shell.

Soon, another friend, Sheldon, wanders over to where we are drinking, eating, and talking. He sees me and says, "Food from the Tree of Life."

I smile and nod.

Spreeboy offers Sheldon a coconut, which he politely refuses.

Sheldon is a "sealed" locksman, one who has formally joined the Ethiopian Orthodox Church. Well read and well spoken, Sheldon begins to speak about the Tree of Life, in Genesis, and how that tree was the same one that blessed the Queen of Sheba. While he speaks, the drummers lay down their jellies and pick up their drums, and the sound of rain on goatskin comes back and everyone smiles.

The song of tree frogs rests on top of the drums. This, along with the big backbeat of the sea, the bass that never rests, is the whole orchestra except for the singular bark of the croaker lizards, a sound not unlike a sudden clap of hands or perhaps two hands striking a couple of flat rocks together.

In any case, it is all music, roots music, as they say, nicer sounding

than what is being played inside the house. Sheldon is talking over the
night music, laying down bars of deep, poetical voice strophes, so that
he, too, is playing an instrument, a thing of subtlety, for, above all else,
Sheldon is an orator, and he knows this and polishes his thoughts pub-
licly whenever he is of that mind.

"Which one is the Tree of Life?" I ask Sheldon. "Everybody says it
is something different."

"Well," he says thoughtfully, with a shake of the head, "The Tree of
Life is anything that bears the fruit of which we partake and live. But
as David, the prophet, declared, 'God Reigneth in the wood.' What that
means is that the Queen of Sheba was blessed by the wood of the tree
of Paradise, and that it healed her cloven foot. Do you know the story?"

I say that I have heard something of it, but not the whole thing.

"I don't remember how Sheba got the cloven foot—was she born
with it?"

Sheldon responds sharply. "It was a devil thing, a magic worked
by the devil. She was a pretty Abyssinian girl, remember. And she was
walking one day when she saw a dragon coming toward her. Now this
same dragon was seen and executed by some holy men, some Ethiopian
saints, they were. I won't go into that now, but, just as the creature died,
a drop of dragon's blood spotted the foot of that girl. And her foot,
the one that was thus struck by evil blood, turned into a goat's cloven
hoof. Now when she returned to her village, it became known that the
dragon was dead. And as it had previously been ravaging their town, the
people honored the girl for killing it, and they made her their queen.
And that is how she came to be known as the Queen of Sheba, which
was the country of her birth."

"Sheldon, where did you learn that legend?" I ask.

Sheldon's voice drops an octave. He replies, "No, legend, mon."

"We would call it a myth."

"Truth is what we deal with here; just truth. The elders of the
Church read Amharic and they know the holy books of Ethiopia, and
they teach us what they know so that we will also know it. For a long
time now, we black people have listened to nursery rhymes like 'the dish

jumped over the spoon.' We have heard about the so-called great pirate Henry Morgan who, so they told us, was a fine statesman, a good governor, and overlord here in the colony of Jamaica. He was, in fact, none of those things: he was a pirate working for the Queen. So, now we are seeing the truth with our own eyes and hearing it with our own ears. To feel it is to know it, that is the only way. Finally, we are feeling our history. This knowledge, my friend, will change human history as we know it. For it is not 'his story' but our story, that of black people everywhere. Seen?"

"But what happened to Sheba's foot? Did it remain deformed?"

Sheldon asks, "Do you think Solomon the King would have allowed such a thing to pass before his eyes unhealed?"

"The way I heard it, he healed her himself."

Now it is his turn to ask me where I heard that and I explain that I have been reading The Kebra Nagast.

"Ah!" Sheldon rumbles. "That is a great book, one of our greatest Ethiopian works."

"Unfortunately, though, I do not remember exactly how the queen was healed."

"It is not in the book. It is a story from Ethiopian oral tradition. Well, I can tell you that when she stepped over the threshold of his palace, she was instantly healed of her deformation."

Sheldon snaps his fingers. "Just like that!"

"The *threshold* healed her?"

"Well, to understand this, we must go back to when Solomon was first building his palace. He could find no stone masons whose art would cut through the giant blocks of stone that he required. So he sent some of his workers into the mountains and they captured a young eagle there, as he had instructed them. This bird was placed by Solomon under a brass pot. Yet the wings were so large they poked out from under the pot. Now the mother eagle, seeing her young one thus caught up, flew over to Eden and took from a tree there a piece of wood, which she carried back to Solomon's courtyard. Dropping the wood from the air, she passed over the brass pot that almost, but not quite, concealed her offspring. Now, that small piece of wood, when it struck the pot that held the bird captive, broke apart. The mother eagle then claimed what was hers, her child. But she left the wood where it fell and returned with her young to the nest. And that wood is the very thing that King Solomon gave to his head stone mason to build his palace and shelter the Ark of the Covenant. That wood was sacred, a gift of God. When the mason put it upon the most obdurate stone, the rock gave way, as if cleaved by the Father Himself. And so it is, and so it shall ever be in the name of the Most High, Selassie I, King of Kings, Lord of Lords, Conquering Lion of the Tribe of Judah. Jah, Rastafari."

Night after night, the drums ring true. But there comes a night when the drummers are there and the drums are not. So some of the men go into the kitchen and bring pots and pans and they assemble a group of *burra* drummers, with the notes high, medium, and low; *akete, funde,* and bass. I find myself on the akete, making the ping, ping tenor tones.

Long into the night we drum, and some sing "By the Waters of Babylon" and other songs. It is early morning, the sky turning to the color of lead, when the pots and pans are put away. Jah Son asks me, "Where did you learn to drum that good?"

"In high school," I tell him. "I took drum lessons and after that, I joined a band."

"Is that when your skin darken up so?"

Mackie laughs when he sees my surprise. "The soot," he tells me, "come off the pot and on to your hands. Between songs, I see you rubbing the sweat off your face with your sooty hands. Now you are black like us."

Later, swimming with Mackie in the sea, he sees me washing my face clean with the salt spray. "We all come black in the beginning, all life start in Africa. So doesn't matter what a mon's face say. So long as his heart speak red blood."

6

Samson

Then Samson went down and his father and his mother,
to Timnath, and came to the vineyards of Timnath:
and, behold, a young lion roared against him.
And the spirit of the Lord came mightily upon him, and
he rent him as he would have rent a kid, and he had
nothing in his hand: but he told not his father or his
mother what he had done.
And he went down and talked with the woman; and she
pleased Samson well.
And after a time he returned to take her, and he turned
aside to see the carcass of the lion: and, behold,
there was a swarm of bees and honey in the carcass
of the lion.

JUDGES 14:5–8

The name "Samson" is sacred to Rastafarians in Jamaica because of
the mythical locksman whose power is nullified by the loss of his hair.
Once this was accomplished by his deceitful Philistine lover, Delilah, as
the Kebra Nagast and the Bible inform us, Samson suffers the fate of all
men made impotent by a woman: he becomes powerless.

Once, he could snap a bowstring like cotton thread, break a new rope like a strand of spiderweb, but now, hairless and enchained, he is helpless as a babe. Eyeless in Gaza where he has been carried away by the Philistines, his enemies, Samson suffers ignobly as the people taunt and make fun of him. However, he is chained between two pillars, which hold up the palace, and, as there are three thousand of his enemies in attendance, Samson asks the Lord to grant him one last grace: vengeance on his enemies. The prayer is granted, and Samson, in a triumphal expression of superhuman strength, pulls down the pillars of the Philistine palace, causing the roof of the temple to collapse, killing everyone, including himself.

Why is this myth so important to Rastafarians? Because of the hair motif thus symbolized. Obviously, one of the most crucial codas of the traditional Rasta is keeping the locks from comb, scissors, or razor. This stems directly from the old Hebraic laws of nondefilement, as redefined in recent years by certain members of the Ethiopian National Congress: "We strongly object to sharp implements used in the desecration of the Figure of Man; e.g., trimming and shaving, tattooing of the skin, and cutting of the flesh."

Proof of Samson's power regained comes at the end of Judges 16 when he prays to God for vengeance, promising his life in the balance. Rastas are fond of pointing out how Delilah soothed Samson, stroking his head on her lap; then, when he fell asleep, calling in a barber to cut off all of his hair. Hairless and powerless, he then becomes eyeless, as the Philistines gouge out his eyes to make him blind. So, the conclusion for the Rastafarians is that a man must remain true to his roots: hair and spirit combined.

The Rastafarian use of Samson as a figure of living folklore comes from the insistence that hair is a kind of power; regard the '60s' habit among Rastas of "flashing dreads," or throwing the head from side to side to send the arrow-like cords in all directions. Bob Marley told his brethren to keep culture, be unafraid of the vulture. Grow your dreadlocks and don't be afraid of the wolf pack. He also wrote verses celebrating David slewing Goliath with a donkey's jawbone. I find a version of the old Samson myth—and perhaps proof that it is not a myth at all—in *The Bible Was My Treasure Map* by Paul Ilton.

The author, before World War II, scours the ancient lands of the Old and New Testaments, from Beirut to Beersheba, and from Bethlehem to Bagdad. Using a combination of intuition and deduction, Ilton finds a golden locust from the time of insect worship; this would be around the biblical time of Solomon's last wife. Searching the Judean hills for artifacts, Ilton finds a story, as valuable in some respects as the antiquities of gold. He discovers on the lips of a sheik the archetypal myth of the great strongman, Samson. The story was told and retold for thousands of years, and according to the storyteller, who, being a Muslim did not consult the Bible, had never seen it written down anywhere, and he told it as if it had just happened.

"Many years ago there lived in these hills a man known for his extraordinary strength. He had the strength of ten men; with one hand he could lift a heavy plow. But he had a single flaw: he was too fond of women. As the years passed his strength grew smaller. This man spent much time in the house of a beautiful widow. But she did not love him; rather she feared him, for he was the enemy of the man she loved. One day the widow asked him what it was that made him so strong, and he answered laughingly: 'My long curled hair.' The next night, in his sleep, she cut his hair, and in the morning showed her true lover into the room. The strong man's strength was gone, and he was murdered like a helpless lamb."

Ilton asks the Sheik who first told him this story. The man replies: "My grandfather, who heard it from his father before him. By Allah, I have not invented it."

> *And what is invention if not beauty?*
> *Every village in Jamaica has a Samson.*
> *Every town has a David.*
> *Every heart has a Solomon.*

7

Jonah

And the whole earth was of one language, and of one speech.
And it came to pass, as they journeyed from the east that they found a plain in the land of Shinar; and they dwelt there.
And they said to one another, Go to, let us make a brick, and burn them thoroughly. And they had brick for stone and slime had they for mortar.
And they said, Go to, let us build a city and a tower, whose top may reach unto heaven; and let us make a name lest we be scattered abroad upon the face of the whole earth.

GENESIS 11:1–4

But he answered and said unto them, An evil and adulterous generation seeketh after a sign; and there shall be no sign given to it, but the sign of the prophet Jonas:
For as Jonas was three days and three nights in the whale's belly; so shall the Son of man be three days and three nights in the heart of the earth.

The men of Nineveh shall rise in judgment with this
generation, and shall condemn it: because they
repented at the preaching of Jonas; and, behold, one
greater than Jonas is here.
The queen of the south shall rise up in the judgment with
this generation, and shall condemn it: for she came from
the uttermost parts of the earth to hear the wisdom of
Solomon; and, behold, one greater than Solomon is here.
When the unclean spirit is gone out of a man, he walketh
through dry places, seeking rest, and findest none.

MATTHEW 12:39–43

Roy knows more about the Bible than any Rasta in the village of Castle Gordon, and, not surprisingly, Roy doesn't read or write. He knows the Bible from having heard it read, or recited, by others. The thing is that Roy has the Bible in his heart from living it, one day at a time. In a sense, he *is* the Bible; he is a walking version of it.

One day Roy is doing a retelling of the story of the Tower of Babel. "There was a time," he says, "when we lived in peace and harmony. This lasted until the Tower. You know the story?"

"I know one version of it."

"There was a time, y'know, when all-a-we, *unu,* just live good like brother and sister, and dem speak the same language, and no separation between one man and another."

"This was in the beginning, before the fruit of the tree of knowledge, and after the Flood," I tell him.

He nods and says, "Money and vanity. Dem two the worst evils and when the people dem build up the great tower so dem could a-reach up fe see the Father, dem was showing Him that money and vanity were good faith, and dem ting got dem there. And dem ting there raise them up to Jah just like you and me face one another now. Just like today human being find a way fe tek us out to dem far reach of the star and planet dem. What vanity live inna de mind of man."

Roy leans against the willow overlooking the sea, his back fitting into the curvature of the tree. His locks fall over his shoulders. He has, if he wishes, the face of Jesus, and, for a moment perhaps, I have a vision of a patriarch untouched by time. For he speaks as if he were in the city of Nineveh, or as a man soon to be swallowed by a great fish.

"No mon," Roy says, "ever see that face. Nuh Moses, nuh Solomon, nuh Abraham get close nuff to burn him face in dat light. No, sah. That don't happen."

"How does it go?" I ask. "Something like the harder we try to get to the Father, the harder we fall, the harder we fail until we let go and know, not believe but know, that the Father is within." Fire said that to me, as well as others, and Roy likes hearing it, and he offers me his fist and we touch knuckles.

"How you know that verse?" he wants to know.

"Well, many people speak; I listen. I do read the Bible. How do you know the things you know, Roy?"

"I know them . . . from Creation."

"Do you mean yours? Or the world's?"

"Both."

"You mean from your own time of birth *and* from the beginning of time?"

"Seen."

"Hmmm. You were there then, at that time?"

Roy raises himself from the tree, eyes alight. "Yah, mon. We all was there then." For a while he stands in the wind, not speaking. Then, "I was born," he whispers, "in the veil of Jah, and when the Tower was built, I saw it with my own eyes. Before slaves laid the stone pon the road dem dig, before the mon Columbus, before the pirate Morgan, before all a dem merchant pirate of England and America and before the Arawak Indian, the Carib, the Egyptian mummy inna him casket of silk, before the president Theodore Roosevelt give to we, poor likkle Jamaica, big bribe ship of carrion beef back inna the first world earthquake of nineteen hundred seven. I was there before the Maroon warrior and the people dem like Nanny, Paul Bogle, and Tacky, and all dem hero dem who fight fe human right and resist colonial rule. Before any of dem ting, I was alive inna de time of locust, inna de time of the winds of Nineveh. Dem call me by another name."

"What was that name?"

"Jonah of Jamaica."

Roy's face is furiously serious. He does not laugh or smile. With great dignity he goes on in this elegiac spoken-verse kind of way, which, I understand, is the product of hearing the Bible and other books read to him but mostly his ear has captured the sound of elders: the flow of their river of words. If, for instance, Fire is the ultimate preacher, then Roy is the premier poet of storytelling. Without the benefit of interpretation, of schooling, of any kind of erudition except pure reasoning among the brethren, Roy has inserted himself into some mystic sphere of time where whatever he says sounds believable. Nor does it matter if it is or it isn't. He goes on and I continue to listen, wondering where it will end up because Roy is a man who loves theme, who follows a current of thought without respite until he has reached a solid conclusion.

"The Tower dem mek was Vanity, and pon the idle hour—what dem call it? Ah, the Coronation of Vanity then was a time when the Father knock it all down and mosh it all up. And from that time forward, *unu* talk in tongue, inna different language. From that time forward, we change up so it all different. Each mon and ooman haffa different religion, a different talk, a different way of doing de same ting. So, no one ting link up wid another. And it is all about corruption, idleness, vanity. And that what destroy us now, what *nyam* each and every one of we down to de bone is this . . ."

I break in for a moment and ask if the Tower of Babel is responsible for the mess the world is in?

Roy kisses his teeth. "As it seh inna de Bible. But lissen me now, I was speaking, y'know, bout me name."

"Oh, yes. Jonah."

"Nuff name man has got!" he cries, shaking his dreadlocks in the sun. "Some call me Jonah, others seh Jehosophat. Some seh Nazarite.

Some seh Dread. But all a dem the same. I come from a long time. I go far forward into the future. I have my home in the ear of corn. And in the Palace of the Pharaoh. I have sung hymns inna the belly of the whale. And as the Father seh fe Moses, 'I am that I am.' Overstand?"

"Seen. You are saying that I-and-I means forever, from the beginning to now, and well into the future. We are what we are, and time makes no impression on us because time doesn't really exist, we just think it does, and if God is truly within man, then man is immortal, and our origins are but moments old."

Roy's eyes gleam. "You overstand," he confirms. "Where you get dat nice scripture?"

"Fire, when I was up at Annotto Bay."

"Ah. Him should know. Was a preacher, y'know."

"Roy, tell about Jonah, I mean, you and the whale."

"What of it?" He stares at me with curiosity. Maybe he thinks I am kidding him.

"You don't know it?" he asks.

"No. That's why I want you to tell me."

"Well, y'see, dat big old fish is of *this* generation."

"You mean right now."

"Don't y'know? If mon can go back in time, mon can go forward too. Time don't change. Time like de sea. Dangerous. Calm. One way or the other."

"The fish is of *this* generation," I repeat.

"Yah, mon."

"So, a giant whale, is that what you say?"

"Dat what you tink?"

"Seems logical to me."

"No, mon. The whale come like nuclear submarine." He raises his voice.

"You are saying Jonah was swallowed by a sub?"

"Anyone could swallow by such an animal of steel . . . common ting, mon. Many brethren go under the sea. It all vanity, but men dweet—

nuh inna Jah name—but in dem own name as them call themselves
Navy, Army, Air Force, CIA, and such."

He lets this sink in for a moment.

"So," he starts again. "Mek we seh I am at war with the Father, that
I refuse fe do his works, then . . . where shall that take I?"

I shake my head.

"Let we seh then I go to Hell on earth. Where would that be?"

I take a lucky guess. "Haiti?"

"The poorest place in all de hemisphere. Yah mon. The people dem
inna Haiti commit all kinda voodoo blasphemy. The star burn up over
Haiti and drop their ash on the people head dem. Cho! I mon alive and
me get belch out the belly of a steel whale, but I refuse to preach fe the
people dem. So, a kind fisherman tek pity pon me and him ferry me to
Cuba, where I see a whole heap of different misery. In Cuba the people
dem are in a spell under the sun. Then I hear the Father whisper inna
me ear: 'Tell the people what will come if they do not mind my word.'

"But, again, I refuse the father and once more catch a ride, this time
on a ganja boat and I get all a way over to Miami where I get a lock-up
inna camp of refugee and dem look dead like duppy. There I see the
Israelites, of which I am one. Dem are the dispossessed out of Egypt.
And I seh unto dem, 'If you mend your way then the Father will set you
free from bondage.' Well, them, at first, ignore me, because, as me did
seh, after the Tower, no one overstand anymore. All is mix-up, mix-up.
But, in time, de people dem lissen what me seh. Why? Cause the Father
arrange it so. Dem begin fe hear with the heart not the ear. And I tell
the people dem that the Holy Zion is within the heart; and they listen.
I tell them that a great wind soon come but dem will spare and not be
hurt. Dem did ask, 'What direction dat wind a-come?' And me seh, 'It
a-come fe Miami, cause that city come like Nineveh now.'"

"That wind was Hurricane Andrew?" I ask.

"And Gilbert and Allen and Hattie, and all a dem . . ."

He nods his head, leans back against the putty gray willow tree.

"The Father slow to anger, but when Him wroth it topple the Tower
of Babel, it lop off the city of Miami."

"So—that is what *could* happen, what *did* happen—what *will* happen if we don't wake up and live."

"Happen before, will again." Roy says.

"And did the Father strike the refugee camp?"

"No, mon."

"Why not?"

"Him see de light inna dem and know de light shall live for-I-ver," he whispers.

Roy yawns, then rests his forearms on his knees. By his bare feet are a bunch of cowrie shells he has collected from the sea. His large hands rest on his bony knees.

I leave Roy there, leaning against his willow tree, falling asleep.

As I walk away, I look back at him again. And I imagine him rowing some great antique wooden boat, resting and rowing, slowly pulling toward Nineveh, an island just over the horizon, a place where the people's heads are ashen and the carcasses of cars rust in the tropic sun like the hollow husks of the pharaoh's locust.

8

Rock

Lord, who shall abide in thy tabernacle, who shall dwell
in thy holy hill?
He that walketh uprightly, and worketh righteousness,
and speaketh the truth in his heart.

PSALMS 15:1–2

Unto thee will I cry, O LORD my rock; be not silent to
me: lest, if thou be silent to me, I become like them
that go down into the pit.
Hear the voice of my supplications, when I cry unto thee,
when I lift up my hands toward thy holy oracle.
Draw me not away with the wicked, and with the workers
of inequity, which speak peace to their neighbors, but
mischief is in their hearts.
Give them according to their deeds, and according to the
wickedness of their endeavors: give them after the
work of their hands; render to them their desert.

PSALMS 28:1–4

Yea also, as lively stones, are built up a spiritual house,
an holy priesthood, to offer up spiritual sacrifices,
acceptable to God by Jesus Christ.
Wherefore also it is contained in the scripture,
Behold, I lay in Zion a chief cornerstone, elect,
precious: and he that believeth on him shall not be
confounded.
Unto you therefore which believe he is precious: but unto
them which be disobedient, the stone which the
builders disallowed, the same is made the head of the
corner,
And a stone of stumbling, and a rock of offense, even to
them which stumble at the word, being disobedient:
whereunto also they were appointed.

FIRST EPISTLE OF PETER 2:5–8

King Solomon said, "Thou didst take dead bones and
cover them with bodies; they were motionless and thou
didst give them energy for life. Thy way was without
corruption, and thy face brought thy world to corruption:
that everything might be dissolved, and then renewed,
and that the foundation for everything might be thy rock:
and on it thou didst build thy kingdom; and thou was the
dwelling place of the saints."

THE ODES OF SOLOMON 22:8–9

Here, in Jamaica, everything is a reminder of rock, of the foundation, for we know that the island was pushed up from the sea and is yet curved and crannied with the thrust of primeval pressure. Some twelve hundred feet above the house where we live, there is a cliff of reef rock. At the top of this cliff, wind-blown and thatch-roofed, there is a small African-Arawak house, where a Rastaman by the name of Erroll lives, and has lived, for many years. I jog up the cliff trail, seeing only an occasional goat, until I reach Erroll's where the view of the Caribbean turns lapis, a glittery expanse of aquamarine that tempts the eye. And there, meditating on his rock of ages, is Erroll. Teak-faced and friendly, he is always laughing and speaking about Ethiopian mysteries. Erroll is the host of the rock. For years now he has been beckoning me to go into the Arawak chamber beneath his clifftop aerie. Politely, I refuse. I do not like the feeling of being confined.

Sometimes Erroll is so persuasive, telling me that Egyptian kings have made their residence in the foundation of the tabernacle. There are kings, he says, sarcophagi, amulets, ankhs, mummies, even ancient books of wisdom to be found here.

I question Erroll—in the spirit of friendly reasoning—if he knows how this cave, presumably Arawak, is related to the mystery of ancient Egypt. I wonder if his response might be similar to Roy's.

Erroll seems almost offended that I do not know the secret answer to this mundane question. Out of his pocket he produces a map of the Nile and he places it alongside a burial chamber diagram of a biblical king, and then he reads from a tattered tract of Rastafarian wisdom, one of those many-times folded Rasta broadsheets that is all but disintegrated from use.

The Patriarchs of the ancient Nyabinghi Order are the voices of the cherubim and seraphim of old. The Arawak Indian chanted songs of praise and hymns of beauty acknowledging that all is one foundation, one rock, one blood, one aim, one destiny, as Marcus Mosiah Garvey did say to all. So let the truth ring out across the nations and be the healing of the nations, the seal of the twelve tribes, the open door of the twelfth gate to the New I-rusalem. Let the many rejoice in the one; let us embrace the root that governs us all, Jah Rastafari.

Erroll reads his poem into the wind that blows freely from the Windward Passage to the rock where we are standing. He is content; Erroll is, if I do not understand what he is talking about. Erroll is unity, or as some Rastas say, "Inity" (placing the universal and collective "I" into as many words as will bear it), and he does not care who is with, or without, him. He cares that he is true to I-self.

I get what Erroll is saying. He, like Roy, is reminding us that the world of the ancients, whether Amerindian or Ethiopian, whether Anglo-Saxon or Israelite, is of one consciousness. Time is irrelevant. It has no power over event because the Father can take it all away in an instant.

To prove his point, he takes me up above the rock to a place where the guinea grass grows uncropped, unmolested by machete or goat. He lifts a cover of grass from the hillside, exposing the dirt beneath. Amazed, I see bones and shards of painted and incised pottery protruding from the dark sandy loam.

"All of this," Erroll tells me, "is Arawak."

I catch a glimpse of Zemis, the little godhead tikis of the Arawak. I see the white rain-polished femurs, clavicles, and smoothly articulated joints of centuries-old bone.

"It is all here," Erroll remarks, "and the cave of the Egyptian solstice down below where my house is watches over it."

Just then, on the hill above us, two hikers come trundling down the narrow goat trail and stop to admire Erroll's finding. I imagine he will cover up the gravesite, let the grass hide it as before, but instead he tells these two English tourists the same thing he has told me. He even recites his script once more but it is all happening quite fast—the gleam of bones, the rapid patois, Erroll's ebullience—and the tourists sort of back up a bit before they realize the significance of the site they are standing on.

"Is this really an Arawak burial mound?" the fair-haired woman asks incredulously.

I explain that it probably is just that.

"How do you know?" she says suspiciously.

I explain that the Zemis that I have just glimpsed and the large food dishes, some of them completely intact and angling out of the pebble-studded earth, are certainly Arawak.

"And how do you know?" she demands, "Are you an anthropologist?"

I tell her that I am a folklorist. And that, yes, I have learned to see things from an anthropological point of view from years of training and study, not to mention apprenticeship.

The woman is still hesitant of the whole thing. She asks Erroll if it is all right to have a closer look.

He says, "Sure."

I warn her that it might not be a good idea.

"Why not?"

"The Arawaks don't like it."

Ignoring me, she kneels down in front of what appears to be a bone-white skeletal hand reaching out of the crumpled soil.

"I wouldn't touch that," I tell her.

Her husband shrugs. "What's the harm?"

I glance at Erroll, who is amused by the attention. The woman edges nearer, and, to get a better look, stands atop a rock, which suddenly crumbles under her feet, spilling her backward into a macca bush.

Later, after we have removed the thorns from her leg, she asks me how I knew that something untoward was going to happen.

Erroll says cheerfully, "He comes up here all the while; he lives up here."

"Then why didn't you stop me when you had the chance?" the woman asks, very much annoyed, glaring at Erroll.

"Nuh me business," he answers, shrugging but still smiling.

I would like to explain to her that Erroll is proud of his little mountainside museum, that he likes to show it to people, but he is not a docent or personal guardian. But instead of saying anything of this sort, I offer her an antidote for her badly swollen leg.

"We'll go down the hill and put 'sinkle Bible' on the macca wounds and they will heal in a day."

This time she does not ask how I know this. We go down hill to our house and garden and stand before one of the largest aloe plants in Jamaica: six feet of exfoliating green leaves reaching out in all directions.

"Sinkle Bible," I explain, "means 'Single Bible' in patois. It will cure just about anything from an impacted colon to a third-degree burn. You can drink it or rub it on your skin. The bitterness of the plant is not in the flesh, but in the outer covering."

I slice a large green leaf and apply the healing medicine liberally.

Two days later the woman stops by our place to show that the deep punctures have healed and there is no scar.

"That Sinkle Bible of yours is a miracle. But just the same, I won't be looking at any more sacred sites," she vows.

I think of Erroll's pride, his Arawak house, his belief that human-kind is one blood, the rock on which his faith is founded.

From where I sit, writing this, I can see the thatch roof of his little house. Soon the Arawak bones will be shipped off to England: word has gotten out, and the official dig will begin in a few weeks.

I think of Erroll's maps and his affirmation of Egypt under his rock; the glory of the kings of Ethiopia resting there, still undisturbed; the silence of the bones reaching out of the stony soil. Finally, I come to the conclusion that it doesn't matter what logic we use or what mystic rite we employ to reach the datum point of universal love.

We are all brothers and sisters, the bones on the hill are not ours but the earth's, and we are of the earth in the same way, soon to fold in among our relations patiently returning to dust, which is why we must walk carefully, tread softly as my Pueblo friends say, move gently as woman's rain. I should share that thought with the next macca lady, or man, that I meet on the mountain, and then be like Erroll, who cares not what they think of his opinion, for that, too, comes from the earth.

9

Tabernacle

Jesus saith unto them, Did ye never read in the scriptures,
The stone which the builders rejected, the same is
become the head of the corner: this is the Lord's doing,
and it is marvelous in our eyes?
Therefore I say unto you, The kingdom of God shall be
taken from you, and given to a nation bringing forth
the fruits thereof.
And whosoever shall fall on this stone shall be broken:
but on whomsoever it shall fall, it will grind him to
powder.

MATTHEW 21:42–44

Bob Marley of Jamaica, echoing Jesus of Nazareth, said, "The stone that the builder refuse shall be the head cornerstone." This is Jesus rephrased, David remade (see Psalm 118). Bob Marley, as usual, has updated the original proverb and made it useful to the builders of our troubled times. The point is that what we often find rejected, or turned away, by authority, is the thing that we need, the thing necessary for spiritual and physical well-being.

I am meditating on Bob Marley's message while looking, now, at the fallen church of Mother Higgins. The Church of Zion on the hill above the reef on the north coast of Jamaica is a place of lost cornerstones. Mother Higgins is gone, dead. Her church, gray and beaten, stands roofless, smitten by the sun. What is left of her life is seen in her son, Michael, a Rasta who sits before me now, smiling and reasoning.

Michael lives in his mother's house, next door to the broken church. Although he is part Maroon, of the fighting Ashanti stock that defeated the English in Jamaica, Michael is primarily a dreadlock Rasta. His baritone voice carries well, and his size—well over six feet, broad-shouldered, narrow-legged—is impressive. Seated before me, he sprawls under a huge mural of Haile Selassie I. Leaning back against it, Michael seems to have grown out of the art wall himself. And this is *his* tabernacle, not his mother's. She was famous as a healer; he is known as an herbalist and bush doctor, a voice of reason in the many-tabernacled parish of St. Mary.

As dusk filters down around us and the reef froths white in the falling darkness, Michael tells me about the former king of Ethiopia, on whom he is now, literally, leaning. As he speaks, Michael and the Lion of Judah dissolve into the purple gloom of the yard. "You know, he was not just a man," Michael starts off, his voice clear and seemingly bottomless.

"Do you hold with what Bob Marley said about him? You know the quote: 'Selassie I, you can check him so. Cause if him eighty-three today, tomorrow you see him and he twenty-eight. And next morning him a baby, and today him a bird. Yah mon. Jah live! Yah can't kill God.'"

Michael rumbles his assent, then chuckling, tells me: "One time he stood upon a bomb that was thrown by Mussolini. The man just stood upon it, and by doing this, he defused it."

"What of the apple?" I ask. "A lot of Rastas speak of how the Emperor cut up an apple in front of King George of England. Do you know the story, Michael?"

"Well, that apple, now . . ."

Michael stretches his nearly seven-foot frame in the cool light of dusk. He is still wearing the soccer uniform, having only recently returned from a match in town.

"The way I hear that one, him toss the apple into the sky. Then him render it into thirteen pieces before it ever touch the earth."

"Render it—how?"

Michael says, "With a sword well-sharp."

I ask Michael what the number thirteen might mean.

He answers vaguely, "Could be the lost tribe of Israel, or maybe the thirteen months of the African calendar . . . ours of the Western world is Roman, you know."

Michael wants the number ignored and the act consecrated.

"What him do, the important thing."

I ask if I can see the healing spring where his mother baptized so many people in the parish, and where she also healed the sick.

We walk down the hill in the amethyst light. The healing spring is like an eye, blinking in the dusk, the banana dark. I peer down over the cliff edge. The spring twinkles in the early starlight. Bending down low, Michael dips his hand, beckoning me to do the same. The water is silky soft, cool.

"Always fresh," he beams, "it never go dry."

Above us in the failing light, the old church is visible, hanging haggardly over the hill. I try to imagine the mile-long procession of parishoners, and Mother Higgins, head topped in the old-style white chignon of Africa, anointing them with holy water amid the outcries of absolution and redemption.

However, Michael's stature is so large it blots even the imagination of another person on the horizon. He is so viably a church unto himself that I forget the past on his premises, and stay with the present. The image of his mother fades. We go back up the trail.

He leads me out onto the road, his broad back pressing against the encircling shadows. Michael is so shoulder-square, so trim of hip that he must walk at an angle to pass between the shanties on either side of the path. His soccer socks are glowing whitely, his legs tapering down darkly into his cleated leather shoes.

"Michael, how is your team doing?" I ask, as we reach the road.

"You must come to our next match: Rasta against Babylon."

He means that his team, the Rastafarian Brotherhood, will play against the local police force team, affectionately known as "Babylon."

I tell him that I would not want to miss it, and we part company there on the Port Maria Road.

A couple days afterward, it is the night of the match. As things turn out, Michael does not get to play. One of his brethren is hurt on the field, and Michael rushes him to the hospital, returning just as the game concludes.

"It doesn't matter," he tells me when we see each other on the road again. He is grinning as always, his voice lowering for emphasis. "Just so everybody is all right."

In Michael's hearty good looks, his great height, and strong posture one can see the vitality of Mother Higgins and her lifelong work to heal others. Her church, hanging on the headland hill, is still there surrounded by sea grape. The hurricanes have taken little sanctuaries of the Lord but hers remains solid. Yet Michael is her tabernacle now, and well he knows this, blessing people on the road with his grin, giving out, as he puts it, "nothing but good vibrations everywhere I go . . . even the wiss and the quit, the vine and the bird, nod to the I and sing praises as I give them back what they give unto me."

10

Revelation

But when they saw him walking upon the sea, they
supposed it had been a spirit, and cried out:
For they all saw him, and were troubled. And
immediately he talked with them, and saith unto
them, Be of good cheer: it is I; be not afraid.

MARK 6:49–50

Spreeboy, whose given name is not known to anyone in Castle Gordon, is a Rastafarian elder. A man of vision, his flesh is drawn against his face like a knot. Spreeboy is probably eighty-something, no one knows for sure. However, he can hop up a sixty-foot coconut palm, as I was saying in an earlier chapter, and drop coconuts the same way he did when he was fourteen. His dreads are gray now, but his eyes, a greenish cat's eye color, are clear; he says it is because he smokes weed. (Most Rastas will tell you that herb prevents glaucoma.) Spreeboy tends a small farm in the town of Mason Hall, located in the hills above Castle Gordon. Once or twice a week, he shows up with a black "scandal bag" full of jackfruit, alligator pear, pine (pineapple), ripe banana, soursop, sweetsop, and guava.

For these gifts of love, Spreeboy refuses money, but, in keeping with some old rite, he will accept tobacco, batteries, and lighter fluid.

One day Spreeboy announces that since I am a writer—a scribe as he phrases it—he wants to tell me history; that is, his story. He begins, as I put pen to paper, not with the incidental factotum of birth, but with a vision of Haile Selassie I.

Sitting in an Edwardian-style bamboo chair in the thatch-roofed outbuilding-bar at Blue Harbour, Spreeboy sits before me like an Ashanti duppy. He is a remarkable-looking man. Nothing about him suggests the present, only the distant past. His pale eyes seem greenish gold, his skin is the color of light coffee. Spreeboy's face, an image of wild concentration, is ever on the verge of humor and moral outrage.

He looks, without trying, like a biblical prophet. Yes, here is a mad-eyed son of the Ethiopian sand, if there ever was one. Yet his eyes are the orbs of fascination for anyone who sees him; he is a deeply hypnotic man. He is also perhaps the oldest Rasta in the area. What he could tell, if he wanted to tell it . . . but now he begins:

"This happened long ago, well before the visit of the Emperor to Jamaica, which was in April of 1966."

Momentarily, his cat's eyes shine in remembrance. His expression turns inward, as if he is not really there but somewhere else, and, when he begins again, his voice rapturous, his eyes aglow, he is very far off, it seems to me, in another world: the world of mythology.

"It was a land of brilliant sun that I recognized, though I knew I had never been there in the flesh."

His voice purrs with a velvety softness. He goes on, eyes tranced, voice dropping to a whisper.

"As I say, the sun was brilliant but it carried no heat. My face turned to the northeast; there the Emperor was, and he took three steps to the left and held up his fist in which he clenched a length of rope. 'Marvel not,' he said. Then, 'Go and read Revelation 5 and 6.' And that was all that he said at that time."

"Did you waken after that?"

"When I became awake, I hurried to the King's Street Bible Museum in Kingston. There was a Bible there that I could read, and this is what it said."

And I saw in the right hand of him that sat on the throne a book written within and on the backside, sealed with seven seals.

And I saw a strong angel proclaiming with a loud voice, "Who is worthy to open the book, and to loose the seals thereof?"

And no man in heaven, nor on earth, neither under the earth, was able to open the book, neither to look thereon.

And I wept much because no man was found worthy to open and to read the book, neither to look thereon.

And one of the elders saith unto me, Weep not: behold, the Lion of the tribe of Judah, the Root of David, hath prevailed to open the book, and to loose the seven seals thereof.

Spreeboy breathes deeply before continuing his recitation of the sixth chapter of Revelation.

And I saw when the Lamb opened one of the seals, and I heard, as it were the noise of thunder, one of the four beasts saying, Come and See.

And I saw, and behold a white horse: and he that sat on him had a bow; and a crown was given unto him: and he went forth conquering and to conquer.

And when he had opened the second seal, I heard the second beast say, Come and see.

Now pausing and looking at me, Spreeboy wants to know if I am following what he is saying.

"I follow it well," I tell him.

He nods.

"Good," he says. "You know Revelation?"

"The Book of the Apocalypse. The end of the world, the beginning of the new order. Alpha and Omega, the beginning and the end."

Spreeboy grins; he looks pleased.

"Shall I continue?"

"Please."

He goes on, "It is the Emperor himself who is loosing the seals, and telling us what is to come. In my vision he is clothed in a golden knit shirt, milk white short pants, and there are two wound-scars on the inside of his palms."

"The same scars," I add, "that Bob and Rita Marley saw when the Emperor came to Jamaica."

Spreeboy claps his hands together.

"That was the twenty-first of April, nineteen-hundred-and-sixty-six."

The date is etched in his mind, and I realize that he is there now; not here with me, though he is talking with me, and making conversation.

His voice drops into that mesmerizing tone.

"I saw His Majesty's plane appear out of the northeast. And, as the plane came in, it was wreathed in a thick cloud of darkness. Then the darkness was washed away with a flood of water. When the airplane started to descend, there was light."

Spreeboy waits, allowing his words to sink in.

For a while he is quiet, neither speaking nor moving, just staring.

A few minutes pass. I ask Spreeboy if he knows the story of Haile Selassie's meeting with King George; how he cut the apple into thirteen parts.

Spreeboy looks up, surprised.

"Who tell you that?" he demands.

"Michael Higgins."

He seems to think about this for a little while.

"There is more to that, you know. More than Michael tell you."

Then he elaborates, telling me, "King George tossed that apple, and with his sword, divided it into twelve sections in the air. When it was the Emperor's turn, His Majesty tossed the apple, cut it up, midair as before, but one section of apple, the thirteenth piece, was stuck to the point of his sword."

"The twelve tribes, plus one."

Spreeboy nods, saying, "Ah!"

"But now," he continues, "I must tell you how the Emperor was received by the big shots of Jamaica. As you must know, he was the first king to ever set foot in an eighteenth-century building on the island of Jamaica. His words bear witness to what happened there at that time, for he said clearly, and for all to hear: 'How can a man resist such an invitation of love and compassion?' He then asked for the Minister of Justice and nobody called forth this minister, so Justice was not there."

Spreeboy wants me to think about this, so he stops talking.

After the appropriate silence, I ask him if the Emperor was speaking in English.

He responds quickly. "He spoke in Amharic, a language we could not understand because those words had long ago been beaten out of us."

"What else did the Emperor say to the people?"

Again, Spreeboy's eyes go off to some point in time, far away.

"His words yet ring in my ears," he expresses poetically. "The Emperor said only one more thing, but I will remember it until the day that I die. He said, 'Holy priests, be still and realize that I am He.'"

For a long while, he is quiet. A car horn on the road seems oddly out of place as does the static pulse of a nearby radio.

After a long, meditative silence, he stands up.

"I will come back another time, and tell you of Marcus Mosiah Garvey," Spreeboy announces, and then he says goodbye in a small, soft voice, and leaves by the back gate. I watch him go down the road, back straight, eyes ahead, his age concealed to all.

As I watch him disappear, I wonder to myself if the magi of old looked and talked like Spreeboy. Somehow, I imagine that they did. But then he casts a spell, which is not of this time or this place. He wraps something around the listener, some subtly woven mesmerism that enables the attentive ear to go on a voyage with him. The words of the voyage are so well chosen, they are like a raft upon the flood. Deep into the middle passage of dream, he takes us, ferrying us through the watery world of myth, and finally, setting us safely on the shore, bedazzled and famished for the next trip. Walking away, however, he resumes the form of an old man whom no one notices under the shade of the almond trees.

11

Never Run Away

Sing unto the Lord a new song, and his praise from the
*   end of the earth, ye that go down to the sea, and all*
*   that is therein; the isles, and the inhabitants thereof.*
Let the wilderness and the cities thereof lift up their
*   voice, the villages that Kedar doth inhabit: let the*
*   inhabitants of the rock sing, let them shout from the*
*   top of the mountains.*
Let them give glory unto the Lord, and declare his praise
*   in the islands.*

ISAIAH 42:10–12

Mackie McDonough is a Rasta of the first order. An old believer. Locked, loaded, bibled and principled, funny, wise, serious, and sad, father of children, leader of men. Mackie can run, chant, drum, swim, testify, and versify with the best of his generation. And, unlike some, he knows whereof he came, he knows whereto he is going. For Mackie had his heritage in the palm of his hand. He has Ashanti blood, and he knows his roots.

    Mackie's grandmother was a bush doctor from the hills of St. Ann, the birth parish of Marcus Garvey, Bob Marley, and Burning Spear. It was she who first told Mackie of his heritage, that he came up from the Ashanti people. Like the Coramantee and the Yoruba, the Ashanti was a warrior nation of West Africa, and one of the hardest peoples for the English, Spanish, and French to subdue. No wonder that many slaves of Ashanti origin took to the bush and became herbalists, necromancers, diviners, warrior-priests, rebels, and prophets. Along with their Coramantee brothers, the Ashanti inhabited much of the north coast of Jamaica, becoming, as slaves, a potent force in the rebellions prior to the English abolition of slavery in 1834.

Mackie knows his history, his story; and his dark face is a finely carved mask of inscrutable character. He can stare down a stump, as the expression is, and he fears no man or woman, and because of this, he is free to move about fearlessly, unhampered by the vicissitudes of a violent and retributive neocolonial society.

If you know him well, and I do, you realize that Mackie's moods are as variable as the clouds passing overhead or the way the harbor color of the sea goes from blue to green to aquamarine. He can laugh one minute, cry the next, be audacious and bold, silent and reserved.

Moreover, there is an open invitation in Mackie to be like him; to move outwardly as a man, a man of knowledge, a man of courage. They have a way of expressing this in Jamaican patois and it is this: "The mon nuh easy." Meaning, a serious person to contend with, one who will bend, but not yield; one who has not come to bow but to conquer.

I have known Mackie for more than ten years during which time we have been constant friends, though, for a couple years, not due to any wrong intention in either of us, we saw little of each other. But now, as it happens, we see one another often, and, lately, we have been meeting and reasoning for hours on the Bible.

"I once wrote a song with Burning Spear," Mackie tells me.

We are sitting, facing the sea, on a day when the left-over hurricane winds of Roberto are churning up the windward side of Jamaica. The sky is dark, and the sea buffets the cliff and the house, folds back the leaves, and whitens them in the wind.

We have been conversing in the wind for about a half hour, when I ask him if, living in Priory, St. Ann, he grew up with Winston Rodney (Burning Spear) who is from the same town and parish.

"We come up together," he says. "In those days, like today, you have to really look at a man to know who he is, how he will move. You know, you could see someone with dreadlocks, and say, that man's all right because he's Rasta. But unless you really know him, you may be deceived about him. So you have to look into the eyes of each man you meet, and measure him accordingly. In the eyes is the truth, for nothing can hide there. The eyes are the light of the heart."

"So what was the song you wrote with Burning Spear?"

"He called it 'Never Run Away.'"

"What's the song about?"

"Well, in those times, in the early seventies at Priory, where both of us are from, we would see each other from time to time, and we would reason together. And so one time when we buck up against one another, he asked me if I would ever leave Jamaica. You know if I would ever have such an intention. At that time, a lot of people were leaving the island to go a-foreign, make their way in England and Canada. I told him I had no intention of leaving Jamaica because it was my home. He liked that, but now he moved away himself."

Mackie chuckles over the changes that divert a man's life, his point of view.

I mention to him that Burning Spear is one of the greatest advocates of Jamaica.

"He even has a song out called 'Land of My Birth.'"

"You love your culture, wherever you are. Where you go, it goes. But back in those days, thirty years ago, we didn't see it that way. We said, the roots and culture are here, why should we leave them? For you can't—if you're true to your roots—be far from that place where you were born and raised."

"So, Mackie, Burning Spear liked the sound of your phrases?"

"He liked them well enough to use them in that song, 'Never Run Away.' In that song his brother says to him, 'I will never run away.' That was me. The song is about morality, not geography. It's about doing what's right, even if it means hardship will follow."

"And did it? Has your life been hard since then?"

"Life hard, mon. Here, everywhere. I don't complain. I am alive, and I have four kids, you know. There's never enough work to support them. During the years that they were in school, I cut my locks, and though I didn't run away, as I told Spear, I did forsake my birthright, in a way—I cut my locks. For it is said, when a man accepts the Father, he must let the locks of his head grow until the day be fulfilled. The years pass; I grow them back, as you see them now."

I ask Mackie what time was the hardest for him.

"In the mid-seventies, I fell prey to a devil name Cocaine. Thinking I could handle any devil—it is written, Rasta must bow to nobody—thinking I could handle this devil, I played a little. But no man can withstand the way this devil work upon the mind, making you think you can do anything, anything at all. And then you come down hard, crash for real, and break apart."

"So you came back and now you just smoke the herb."

Mackie chuckles.

"Smoking is a part of our religion. It is our cup of blessing, in which we show our avocation of the Lord."

Just as Mackie finishes saying this, a hard rain begins to fall. The white, storm-lashed sea boils over the reef. Watching the waves, Mackie recites a verse from the Bible. Then another. The spray leaps up, a verse comes forth.

"Nothing tell it like the Bible." He grins from within his dreadlock beard.

"What books of the Bible do you like best?"

"Matthew, Isaiah, Ecclesiastes, Revelation."

I tell him, "A lot of Rastas, up-and-coming I would call them because they are young—in their twenties—haven't checked the Bible, don't know what the meaning of life really is. What they know is just what they get from the herb, but that is only a part of it."

"Half the story has never been told," Mackie laughs.

The sea crashes, throwing tiny diamonds into his beard.

"Blessed are they which do hunger and search: for they shall be filled," Mackie says, laughing.

The sea spits white froth on the rocks.

"Blessed are the pure in heart: for they shall see God."

The waves clamor restlessly in the harbor.

"Blessed are the peacemakers: for they shall be called the children of God."

"How about the children of Solomon?" I say.

And Mackie answers with a laugh.

"The children of Solomon are all of us," he proclaims, still amused by the power of the sea, the nature of the storm.

Then he turns and his eyes find mine. "The worst thing I ever did to a man was not to answer him."

"When did that happen?"

"A few years ago."

"Tell me about it."

"I was on the beach at Priory and a man came up to me with a grievance in his face. He reviled me, he did. He persecuted me with words, with all manner of false accusations. So I sat him out, but it took all day. Finally, after hours and hours of hurling abuse at me, he stalked off, unsatisfied because, all during that time, I never answered him. Not one single word did I say. I just sat there and stared into his eyes."

I read Mackie the passage from Matthew 5, verse 39, where Jesus says: "But I say unto you, that ye resist not evil: but whosoever shall smite thee on the right cheek, turn to him the other also."

Mackie grins. "It is just so. And, you know, I saw that man who hated me the other day. He walked up to me and he said, 'You did hurt me more with your silence than if you had spoken to me.' So, I answered him back, after all these years."

"What did you say to him, Mackie?"

"I said, 'Judge not that ye be not judged.'"

For at least another hour, Mackie and I sit in silence, watching and listening to the sea. The last thing he said as he got up to go down the road to Priory was, "Never run away. Face whatever it is, and you will always be free."

12

Prophet

> But Jesus said unto them, "A prophet is not without honor,
> but in his own country, and among his own kin, and
> in his own house."
> And he could there do no mighty work, save that he
> laid his hands upon a few sick folk, and he healed
> them.
> And he marveled because of their unbelief. And he went
> round about the villages, teaching.
> And he called unto him the twelve, and began to send
> them forth by two and two; and gave them power over
> unclean spirits;
> And commanded them that they should take nothing for
> their journey, save a staff only; no scrip, no bread, no
> money in their purse:
> But be shod with sandals; and not put on two coats.
>
> MARK 6:4–9

I have been reading about Marcus Mosiah Garvey, Mackie's and
Burning Spear's countryman, a black man who grew up in the sweet
hills of St. Ann some fifty years before they did. Garvey, the prophet of

African roots and repatriation, whose reputation even today is clouded with misunderstanding, was a figure of greatness, but he was also such a complex man that it is difficult sometimes to assess him properly. Some say he was a tormented, gifted, spiritual leader, a man who should have stayed out of politics. Others note that his remarkable qualities came from his passion for, and support of, the political arena that gave him so much grief. What was he, and what is he to us today?

Beside Emperor Haile Selassie I, Marcus Garvey is seen by the Rastafarian community, as a guiding light. His spirit, something like the Holy Ghost to some Rastas, is one of redemptive grace; Garvey taught rootsmen-in-the-making how to find their ancestry; he told them how to become Ethiopian, and he urged them to reconsider their actions in light of their immanent return to the fatherland of Africa.

In the Rasta pantheon there are three notable prophetic figures, whose names are indelible and whose sayings and proverbs are always on people's lips. Therefore, there is a kind of triumvirate, as in the shaping of the Old Testament theology of Moses. If, for example, Haile Selassie I represents the figure of Jah, or God almighty, then Marcus Garvey would function as a biblical patriarch such as Moses (the name fits: Marcus Mosiah). Bob Marley, whose mythology is the newest of the three, seems to be a martyred prophet; some say he is the modern black equivalent of Jesus.

All of this is relative, of course, since Rastafarianism is an atomically principled—that is, constantly changing—religion that does not wish to call itself a religion. So each individual Rasta seems to have his own/her own patriarchal figure(s).

Marcus Garvey, as the prophet of black redemption, is universally admired by the previous generation of Rastafarians. Burning Spear began his career chanting mystic hymns in praise of Garvey, and his anthem is still ringing and one of his thoughtful questions—"Who was old Marcus Garvey?"—is still being answered today.

Among other things, Garvey was the creator, almost single-handedly, of the concept of repatriation. But he also founded the African Orthodox Church of America, the Black Star Line Steamship

Company, the Universal Negro Improvement Association, and *The Negro World* newspaper.

Yet the most important of Garvey's contributions—from a Rastafarian point of view—is his declaration that the exploited Africans of America and Jamaica were actually Ethiopian. The background of this is biblical. All Garvey had to do was quote from it. Malcolm X acknowledged an indebtedness to Marcus Garvey: "The entire Black Muslim philosophy here in America is feeding upon the seeds that were planted by Marcus Garvey."

One of the most interesting myths about Marcus Garvey is that he was actually stoned in Port Maria while giving a speech in the mid-thirties. "Stoned," the people say, "for a bowl full of rice." Another well-known myth concerns a traitor to Garvey, a man named Bagowire. The name comes from the words "bag of wire."

This myth states that Garvey's butler-driver-assistant sold him to the authorities, just as Judas sold Jesus to the Pharisees. Garvey did, in fact, do time in a federal prison in Atlanta, Georgia, for a trumped-up U.S. charge of mail fraud, but the mythologists of Garvey neglect this in favor of the Bagowire legend.

No one knows much about the real character of Bagowire today except that the man ended up a madman on the streets of Kingston, and that he was dressed in paper wrapped with tangles of wire, hence the ironical-poetical name.

Rastafarians have also canonized the tale of Garvey's incarceration in the Spanish Town gaol of Kingston, Jamaica, the place where Bagowire's duplicity supposedly sent Garvey. The false charge resulting in a three-month jail sentence kept Garvey from campaigning for municipal and national offices, thus giving his opponents sufficient time to win the election of 1930.

When Garvey was finally released from prison, he made a proclamation while closing the door of his cell: "This gate shall be shut, it shall not be opened, and no man shall enter in by it." And such, Rastas tell us today, is still the case: the door is locked to all who would try to open it. The Port Maria myth, of Garvey's being stoned in exchange for food probably stems from the same historical period. I find the following quote in a pamphlet on Marcus Garvey.

> Thus, on his release from prison, he had only a few weeks to campaign and was without funds. In the general election for the Legislative Council on January 29, 1930, Garvey lost the rural St. Andrew seat to a white man named Seymour . . . who just happened to be the mayor of Kingston. Despite the limited means and time at his disposal, Garvey's campaign could hardly have been better organized. He lost in the final analysis because the people of Mavis Bank, Content Gap, Guava Ridge, Irish Town, Redlight, Maryland, and Gordon Town surrendered to Mayor Seymour in the rum war and money scramble initiated by him. Garvey lost because voters sold out for a feast in Gordon Town Square of rice and peas washed down with lots of liquor . . . courtesy of the Mayor.

The myth continues along. The story is told that the residents of Gordon Town today suffer from an old curse coming from that short-sighted time. Apparently, even now, their public transportation system does not run effectively, despite the fact they are the nearest rural town adjacent to Kingston. And, if the same curse was promulgated after Garvey was stoned in Port Maria, the effect is somewhat the same. More than sixty years later, this once thriving banana port is a town in shambles, dogged by the direst poverty on the island.

One morning, Spreeboy shows up again with a bag full of pineapples and some stories about Marcus Garvey that have not appeared in any of the books.

"I know the true prophecy," he tells me.

"Which prophecy?" I ask.

Immediately, Spreeboy begins to explain what he knows.

"Marcus said that the people would cry out three times after his death. But he told them not to believe it (his death). The first time the people cried out was when President Tugman came to Jamaica and was greeted by Prime Minister Norman Manley. Garvey appeared in the presence of President Tugman, and a twenty-one gun salute was heard at that time. And so, the people cried out because they recognized that although their beloved Garvey was gone, his spirit now resided in the fleshly form of President Tugman.

"The second time the people uttered a cry was when Marcus Garvey's ash was returned from England where he died in 1940. And the third time the people cried was in 1965 when Garvey's body was laid to rest at Heroes Park in Kingston."

I ask Spreeboy who President Tugman is, but he merely raises his eyebrows, amazed that I am so ill-informed. When I ask him, "How could there be ash, and also, later, a body to bury?" He is equally astonished, and brushes my question aside with annoyance.

"Things are as they are," he chides. Someone else, trying to help, puts in, "What goes around comes around," quoting, once again, Bob Marley. So it is expressly clear, in the context of myth, that Marcus Garvey's prophecy was reshaped and given substance by The New Testament. In Mark 14, Spreeboy explains that Jesus is betrayed by Judas Iscariot, just as Marcus is betrayed by Bagowire, and he quotes the following from Mark 14:27–30.

> And Jesus saith unto them, "All ye shall be offended because of me this night: for it is written, I will smite the shepherd, and the sheep shall be scattered. But after that I am risen, I will go before you into Galilee."
>
> But Peter said unto him, "Although all shall be offended, yet will not I."
>
> And Jesus saith unto him, "Verilee I say unto thee, 'That this day, even in this night, before the cock crow twice, thou shalt deny me thrice.'"

"Do you know of any other of Garvey's prophecies?" I ask Spreeboy.

"There is the time that he predicted our world, turned upside down in chaos, such as you will read about in Revelation."

Roy, who is seated nearby, says, "Didn't I tell you before about that prediction? People throwing money away on the streets; coins filling the gutter because no one wants them."

Spreeboy nods judiciously. "It is so. Marcus said a time would come when the people would bear arms in Jamaica and Bagowire, the traitor said to him, 'Where will the people get such things?' Because, as we know, this was the period of colonial rule when a man got stripes on his back for any insubordination. This was a time when the police themselves carried only whistles and sticks, and no one had any arms, not even the government. Then, in 1976, during the bloody elections of that time, the people bore arms and many were killed; and again in 1987 with Michael Manley this happened again, and it is happening now in Spanish Town and these places where the gangs rule the community. But the men do not rule. It is as Marcus told us, the guns are the rulers and mankind merely the trigger-finger."

Spreeboy has lived in the hills of St. Mary, working a small family-owned farm, ever since the political wars of 1980 when, as he says, "Two thousand people were slaughtered in the streets of Kingston." He remembers well what happened then.

"I saw the arms that were brought in by the Jamaican Labor Party to overcome the People's National Party. The PNP minister, Morgan, lost his life. I lost my house in Spanish Town, and had to flee for my life. But before I could get away, I was backed into my basement by eight gunmen. I hid under a sheepskin in a dark corner and the gunmen didn't see me right away. The Father it was who hid me and saved my life. For those gunmen stalked me, they knew something was down there. Now I had some puppies and they were jumping about on the floor, licking that sheepskin where I was hidden. I said to myself, 'If I should survive this, another election won't find me here.' But, as I say, the Father was watching over me, and one of the hired guns spoke thus: 'Come away, mon. Don't you see it's puppies playing wid him muddeh?' And they left, one after the other, up the stairs. After that I packed my things: I took only a plastic bucket into which I placed my machete, wrapped in newspaper, as if I were going to the field to work. Yet I knew that I was leaving permanently, and I never have returned to that place."

The next day we drive, Ernie and I, to the Parish Library of St. Ann's Bay. There, standing in the sun, is the huge, larger-than-life statue of Marcus Garvey sculpted by Alvin Marriott. He stands implacably in the sun, great-shouldered, big-legged, a solid-looking man. The base of the statue has a plaque that reads "Right Excellent Marcus Mosiah Garvey, National Hero."

As every Rasta knows, Marcus was hounded out of his own country to die as a lonely expatriate in England in 1940. However, here he stands, the National Hero, welcoming us as we welcome him. But the truth was cast some two thousand years earlier by that greatest of castaways, Jesus of Nazareth, when he said: "A prophet is not without honor, save in his own country, and in his own house."

13

Blood

Two are better than one: because they have a good reward
*   for their labor.*
For if they fall, the one will lift up his fellow; but woe to
*   him that is alone when he falleth; for he hath not*
*   another to help him up.*
Again, if two lie together, then they have heat: but how
*   can one be warm alone?*
And if one prevail against him, two shall withstand him;
*   and a threefold cord is not quickly broken.*

ECCLESIASTES 4:9–12

We are in the foothills of the John Crow mountains, swimming in a crystal blue stream, watching children jump off the waterfall, a leap of some thirty-five feet.

The sun is hiding in the clouds and the long withes, or creeper vines, hang from the opaque shadows of the guango, breadnut, mahogany, and cedarwood trees. Over the forest there is cloud cover, yet the sun pours into it, making the verdant earth steam.

I stand at the edge of the falls, a little uncertain about the leap. Then my feet refuse to budge, the rushing water foams around them as I stand there trying to make up my mind. Then one of my students comes up behind me and says, "What, no courage?" That is all it takes. Suddenly, I am in the air arcing over the silver waterfall, heading for the prism of blue beneath my toes.

I am dropping like a stone.

Yet the sensation of weightlessness and suspended animation lasts far too long. My heart jumps into my throat. Miles below the imaginary water glimmers. Then glows. Then, all at once, I am actually falling into the clear depths, fish jazzing about in all directions, as bubbly thing that I am, I descend, stop, begin to rise up in a cocoon of pearls.

Finally, I find myself on the surface gulping air. The jump is over, I am still alive, and I know that I will not have to do it again.

No, I cannot say that it was fun.

There was just too much falling going on.

Afternoon comes lazily to the rainforest part of Jamaica. But when it does, the droplets strike like bullets, muddying the road, buffeting the leaves, and making a roar in the upper branches of the outspread trees. In a matter of minutes, our minibus is mired in a contagion of detritus, which sweeps down from the hills on the coffee-colored tide.

Mackie, who is driving us around that day, tries ineffectually to back up out of the way of the sucking swamp. There are at least fifteen of us in the bus at the time, all students, except Mackie and myself, and no one can imagine what is going to happen next.

Suddenly, the bus slides sideways and begins to roll, righting itself at the last moment, and in time for Mackie to slide open the gliding door, and yell, "Everybody out!"

What follows is like the thunder of elephants. Everyone scrambling like crazy, and diving out the door into the swirling tapioca of mud. As the bus goes off the embankment and rattles, driverless, downhill into an odd cul-de-sac of toppled trees, we swim, if that is the word, for higher ground.

Miraculously, each student makes it out in time, and hits the mud without incident. But the bus is marooned in subterranean ooze. The overcast day darkens, clouds bring more rain. Like wood rats, we scurry about madly, looking for shelter. We are wet to the bone. We are bone-damp, mud-scored, pitiful persons. But who will rescue us but us? For we are miles and miles from *anywhere* that could be called *where*.

We are way out in the John Crows in a tropical downpour, and our bus is a piece of jetsam caught in a log jam. The swamp is a hungry dragon that eats buses. And there is nothing about this day that does not spell disaster.

"So," I say to Mackie while the mud runs off my nose, "we're forty miles from Port Antonio, which is one hundred miles from a tow truck, in the middle of an all-day-downpour and our bus is sunk in mud that looks like shit, and I suppose there's nothing to do but face the music and walk, right?"

The vapors from the swamp are rising, even as I speak, but Mackie, mud-bespeckled as he is, does not seem discouraged.

"No, mon," he says, looking tragically at the scene. But I can see that he is not about to give up on getting that sorry bus out of the mud. Hope is never lost with Mackie, just temporarily misplaced. Out of the driving rain and down-beaten vegetation, grayish forms are gathering that appear to be human. Yes, the shapes of men emerging from the primal steam of the swamp. Some have ropes, others have pickaxes. Some have shovels, others have lengths of chain. Mackie has the machete he always carries with him.

And so, the next thing I know, we are engaged in a primal struggle to free the bus. The rain roars. The girls get all helmet-headed, rain-glossed, their hair so hard to the scalp it looks like shell. The boys wear skullcaps. The mud lacquers our skin, turning us all shades of earthen color. And the color changes as more rain and more mud paints us and washes us clean, and paints us again.

Soon even our eyes are mud-lashed. We grow hoarse with yelling and weak from pushing. We jam shoulders and brace hips, and the infernal bus creaks one prehensile wobble forward. In an hour's time, we are glazed in the many-hued mud. Not one person is the same shade or tone. Not one item of clothing is identifiable. Not one expression is discernible. We are all in this crucible of color.

One body straining, one body of muscle, slowly, painfully dragging a minibus up a hill by chain, rope, bluster, and will.

Night darkens the rain forest. The rain quits. Fireflies spark up the dark. Mackie chips at the rocks that block our passage. Flowers of sparks come with every chip of his cutlass. The rocks give way under the smoking tires; the bus gains another quarter inch.

Who knows how long we labor in this muddy purgatory?

Yet with each surge, the bus inches nearer the road.

More laughing people come out of the hills to help us. The chain of workers spreads far into the night.

And then finally, and comically, hope rides out of the forest on a white donkey.

He looks like an apparition, a Rastaman riding on a snowy donkey. Carrying a sword of light in his right hand—a torch—he comes down the rain-gemmed leafy road into the clearing. The moment we see him, everyone—Americans and Jamaicans alike—start to laugh. It is the funniest thing we have ever seen. The Rastaman dismounts, and he, too, is laughing. At himself. At the way we look. At the rain. At the helpless, foolish minibus.

Mackie says, "Welcome, brother."

And the Rastaman hitches his donkey to the mud-spattered bumper and gives it a pat and a shout, and with that all of us start pushing and giving up one final, communal groan, and the bus squooshes free and slides onto the road. It is done.

A feeling comes over me that can only be described as natural love. A deep gratitude for life, for suffering, sharing and bonding—and most of all—for not giving up.

I feel, though encased in mud, that I, and all the others are like glow sticks: beings with light coming out of us. In no time, however, the people who have come out of the forest to help us have passed back into the forest. It is just Mackie and me and the students, who are now chattering over their great adventure.

It is all moonshine to them.

They go back to the falls for one last cleansing of the skin. A few

Jamaicans build a bonfire by the cymbal-crashing water, and the swimmers come out and warm themselves by the dancing fire.

I muse to Mackie, "Would that I could keep this mud on a little longer."

"No, mon," he says, "what skin deep wash away. What blood deep stay for-iver."

14

Bomb

Blessed is the man that walketh not in the counsel of
*   the ungodly, nor standeth in the way of sinners, not*
*   sitteth in the seat of the scornful.*
But his delight is in the law of the Lord; and in his law
*   he doth meditate day and night.*
And he shall be like a tree planted by the rivers of water,
*   that bringeth forth his fruit in his season; his leaf*
*   also shall not wither; and whatsoever he doeth shall*
*   prosper.*

PSALMS 1:1–3

One summer day Mackie is sitting under a casuarina tree. Beside him is his son, known to family and me as Junior but called Leon otherwise. Mackie's sitting on a cushion of dry pine needles, listening to the wind sighing in the tree and staring off at Cabarita Island while his son does exactly the same thing.

"Hey, mon," I say, coming up to the two of them. Mackie offers me his fist in the old way, and we touch knuckles, and Mackie, serious as always, says, "Those who have eyes must look upon what we see."

I have eyes and I see the grandest of all shade trees, and just below it, a few feet from where Mackie and Junior are perched, still and statuesque, the ancient stone steps lead down to a foamy beach and there the incoming tide plays with a long cylindrical object.

"You see it?" Mackie asks.

I nod. A long frosted-looking tube that looks like . . . a torpedo.

"Is it what I think it is?"

"Yah, mon."

Mackie turns around, sees a kid on a bicycle coming round the double bend of the road from Race Course, and shouts, "Bwai, me find one a dem bomb dem. Tell police fe come quick!"

A shrill voice from the tar road comes back, "Yah, mon," and the boy is off sailing downhill to Port Maria.

We watch him disappear around the corner, a herd of goats blatting displeasure as he weaves among them.

I stare down again at the torpedo. On the sides are these huge black stenciled words:

INCENDIARY EXPLOSIVE PROPERTY U.S. NAVY
IF RECOVERED REPORT TO MILITARY AUTHORITY
IMMEDIATELY

Mackie and Junior are sitting, neither one moving. There is a coolness in their expression, like father, like son. But I am musing over the possibility this is no joke but rather a real live bomb on the Blue Harbour beach and a boy is riding a bicycle to Port Maria to inform "the authority" and otherwise it's just a typical day in Jamaica with fair skies and balmy seas and the hills of pimento trees almost iridescent green on Blackwell Hill.

Sitting with Mackie and Junior, I say as little as they, we three watch john crows sail the thermals high up over the coral heads and the long crawl of white froth on the reef so white it erases the blue. A yellow banana quit hisses a long whisper song in a palm tree whose dead fronds hang in the wind, the tragic effects of lethal yellow, a disease that has killed many of the Jamaica Talls on this part of the north coast. Our silence is over when a Land-Cruiser growls to a stop on the rise above and behind us. Four well-groomed officers step out into the sun glare. Their dark blue trousers have a common crimson stripe up the side and their short-sleeve pinstripe shirts are creased and ironed. They come downhill in their polished black shoes and tidy clothes, and then all four dip into that Jamaican squat, very low to the earth. They, too, study the bomb. In silence.

Mackie doesn't offer them any information and after what seems like a pretty long time, the officers show signs of boredom. Meanwhile the bomb slides forward on the incoming tide, making an eerie tinkling sound as beach pebbles wash over it.

Mackie eyes one of the officers and says in patois, "Wha ya gwan do wid dis ting?" He says it rapid fire. The fat man with the sergeant's stripes shrugs. He has a trim little mustache and a heavy, sad face. "Yuh carry-come down a station," he answers gruffly.

Mackie makes a face at the other policemen. "What de mon say fe do?" he asks.

The lower-ranking officer looks sleepily out across the harbor toward Hurricane Allen Point where a Rastaman has planted a red, green, and gold flag in a pile of reef rocks. The flag is beating back and forth in the wind off Cabarita Island. Finally he pulls his eyes away from the tattered flag, says, "Mon say take that thing, bring down the station house."

"Me?" Mackie says doubtfully. "No me work dis!"

The sergeant turns to Mackie. "You see dat bwai?" he asks.

"Bicycle bwai dat," Junior pipes up.

"Me see de bwai," Mackie answers staring at the flag in the wind and not the boy who is sidled up to us on a very battered bike.

"You de manager?" the sergeant says.

Mackie nods.

"Then you give dis bwai wid de bike de bomb tek fe military like it say on a side a dat ting. No police job dis!"

The bike boy's mouth drops open. He shakes his head.

"Me ride all way down fe military wid bomb on me back?"

All three policemen give the boy a cold, unison nod.

At that moment, Mackie stands up. One second he is seated, the next he is dashing down the stone steps to the beach. Then he hefts the torpedo onto his shoulder, charges back up the stairs, and drawing a deep breath, pitches the bomb off the promontory into the lagoon.

All of us draw a breath, thinking it might be our last.

There is a huge splash, the bomb hits the water and after bobbing up and down, rides the froth of a wave and is thus drawn back to shore where it rolls in the sand, clanks against a rock, and then with the force of the reef-going currents gets sucked out so fast that it seems propelled by its own propeller.

No one says a word. We are just standing there.

But I notice the brows of the policemen are sweaty.

In a low voice, Mackie tells Junior, "Faddeh mek we gift, so me return. Unopen."

Then he laughs once and struts off cockroach style and Junior goes with him three steps to Mackie's one.

For a while the policemen and I stand on the hill watching what appears to be a large silver fish swimming steadily out to sea, turning life-like on the trade-wind pull of the strong outgoing current, turning and rolling silvery and slow, bobbing and moving forward, a crisp lace of whiteness appearing and fading on its gleaming roundness as it goes out from whence it came. I make a note to ask Mackie, if the Father gave the gift, what was he doing in Babylon?

15

Healer

Now there are diversities of gifts, but the same spirit.
And there are differences of administrations, but the same
Lord.
And there are diversities of operations, but it is the same
God which worketh all in all.
But the manifestation of the spirit is given to every man to
profit withal.
For to one is given by the Spirit the word of wisdom; to
another the word of knowledge by the same Spirit;
To another faith by the same Spirit; to another the gifts of
healing by the same Spirit.

I CORINTHIANS 12:4–9

Horace is called "Horace" by people who know him in the village of Albany, Jamaica, but he is known to many of us by the nickname, Winston Churchill. A dreadlock, our Winston looks nothing like the heroic statesman, or his classic cigar, but this Jamaican Churchill is both heroic, in his own way, and also as soft as fine blue smoke on a summer's night. His twinkle-eye and easy smile could charm a snake, and probably have.

Churchill knows about every granny medicine the bush has to offer. I depend on him for such well-known Jamaican tricks as what to do when a sea urchin stings your foot.

"Yuh muss pee on de foot dem." Easy for a guy, harder for a girl—and harder still for a teen boy to pee on a teen girl, especially when she's looking, and mostly she does, but that is what we do here when stung by an urchin.

Churchill shows me how to cure a 40-legger bite.

"You muss tek the 40-legger and don't mosh him up but put him in a bokkle of 100-proof plus, Wray & Nephew white rum. Mek we wait tree month for dat cure fe ripe up nice."

I tell Churchill, "Navajo Indians use the same cure for a centipede bite, but they crush the centipede—and it must be the one that bit the person, not some other happening-along-centipede—and they make a poultice of the moshed centipede and this brings down the swelling and nullifies the poison."

"Pisen?" asks Churchill.

"Yes, pisen."

About one week after Churchill tells me about the 40-legger antidote, I am jogging along a bamboo fence line when I cut my foot on a broken bottle. Jamaicans often break bottles along a fence to keep intruders out, the same way in Mexico they place the jagged bottle-fangs on top of a fence while the cement is still wet, and come to think of it, they do this throughout the Caribbean as well. And now I've gone and stepped on a two-inch piece of dirty glass and my season of teaching the youth to run is suddenly over.

I am on one leg when Churchill sees me, and says, "Mek we cure the foot, Ger." I agree, not only because I believe in Churchill's materia medica, but after all these years I have also come to believe that all things that happen in Jamaica can be healed in Jamaica, and this includes death, since most Rastafarians do not believe in an end to life: certainly not the way we do in the culture at large.

The cure for broken bottle wound in the tender heart of one's foot is not as dramatic as pouring kerosene oil in a bullet wound, and I have seen this done, or the rubbing of a bissy nut on an open sore, but it is nonetheless an experience you would not want to live through twice.

Churchill's hands go to work on cleansing the foot, first.

I am asked to crook my leg at the knee, and while standing under an outdoor spigot, Churchill lets the icy water run over the still bleeding gash. Then he turns off the water and rubs a fresh-cut, halved lime into the two-inch wound, squeezing the juice in and rubbing it in circles. This is followed by pouring salt into the wound, then more running water, then more lime and extra salt.

I am dizzy with the pain, but I stand up to it all right, I suppose.

The last part of the ceremony is where everyone gathers round to see and to comment, and to act out the little diorama of healing. Roy is there, dreads curtaining down, offering encouragement. Dreamy, looking like a judge's screw face, Clover, the Maroon girl six-foot tall, the best runner of them all, hopping on one leg and telling of her own injury, dancing away the pain for my benefit. "You will run tomorrow, Ger," she says, laughing. "Yah, mon, zoom like a likkle small birdie," Roy joins in, chuckling.

I, for one, would like all this drama to be over.

Now Churchill rubs the cleansed wound on the inside—the raw, red laceration as wide as it is deep—with the skin of a green banana. Over and over he applies the whitish, moist banana skin.

"What will this do?" I ask.

"Kill the pain."

"Anything else?"

"Mek yuh walk good."

"How about run?"

"Run like Rasta."

He rubs and he rubs. Then he folds the ripped flap of skin back on, and he places a piece of raw, hard banana skin over the top of the closed cut and ties it down with a pandana string. Lastly, he pulls a clean white sock over my foot and tells me to keep my foot elevated until the morning.

I do exactly what Churchill says to do.

I am lying in bed and wondering what happened to my foot.

I don't feel anything below the ankle.

In the morning, however, I remove the sock and look.

The line where the skin was torn, the flap-line, as you might say, is a faint reddish scar, which looks weeks, maybe months old. In other words, an old forgotten scar. No pain whatsoever in the formerly hurt foot, which I can stand on, hop on, and, yes, believe me, run on.

If this isn't a small, or large, miracle of bush doctoring, what is?

"How we dweet," Churchill says.

Some of the rootsmen in these paintings are still with us but some are gone from Jamaica, and some are gone from the earth. We "livicate" this book to them, as it comes from their minds and hearts "for-Iver."

Craven choke puppy

(Greed is bound to cause a puppy to choke.)

Mackie McDonnough

"Babylon fell because of wickedness and greed." Mackie's point of view was always that community, "I-nity," and love were the values we should cherish. Mackie is the source and substance of this book. He comes and goes in seven chapters because he was our first "grounation" into the Rasta experience, way of life, herbology, diet, and generous way of being one with everything. He was a brother in all senses of the word.

Who de cap fit, mek 'im wear i'

(Whoever is guilty, let him assume that he is being accused.)

Gerald Hausman and Ernie Uton Hinds/who the cap fit
As the bus driver for our school, Ernie drove us all over Jamaica in his minibus named "the Irie One."

Milo the fisherman
Just as the hoe will always find a stick-a-bush to chop, Milo found a fish to catch to feed the students at our school.

Ev'ry hoe ha' dem stick a bush

(To each his own.)

Horace Winston Churchill

Horace taught herbology: all kinds! Farmer, healer, friend, his smile alone could soothe a troubled heart.

Denzel Harrow

When times were tough and the water was scarce, faithful Mr. Denzel brought buckets to us on his head. Many buckets, much love.

Ev'ry rivah runa 'im mumah

White River Bridge
Every river runs to the sea. "Sir-vival" is the game that keeps us afloat.

Stan the wicker man Irons
Stan was the very portrait of patience and tolerance, and he made life look easy when it was all uphill.

Fren' nevah so'easy fe fine as fe lose

Han'some-to-pieces
(Extraordinarily handsome.)

Roy McKay

Looking into Roy's face, one can hear the proverb *"If you want love you must love."* The wisdom of Solomon was in his eyes.

Spreeboy

Spreeboy met Haile Selassie I in Kingston, Jamaica, and was ever so wise in quoting scripture and speaking about Rastafari.

Han' full come, han' full go.

Him dat wan love mus love
(Give to me and I will give to you.)

Roy McKay
Probably more than any other person at Blue Harbour, Roy became the brother, father, friend that everyone knew and shared. He was there in every emergency and saved lives and careers. Roy was the glue that held it all together.

Raggy Anthony Henry
Like the mongoose, Raggy was everywhere, and nowhere, all at once. Hardly anyone could keep up with him in the water or on the land.

Mongoose seh Man who nah tek chance a no man at all

(The mongoose lives by the dictum that a person who does not take chances is not worthwhile.)

Me trow me corn but me no call no fowl

(Throwing out a provocative statement in an indirect manner puts off accusations of personal insult.)

Stephen Marley

The first Marley we met was Steve. He was a boy, but like all of Bob's sons and daughters he was wiser than his years. Today, it's in his music.

Benji Brown

(right) was as cautious as he was careless. He learned to watch everything because, as he said, "Everything has life."

Mongoose seh risk no man, even if him cannot run

(Mongoose says not to take chances with a man, even one who cannot run.)

Rain never fall on one man house top alone

Bob Marley's birthplace

Bob's birthplace reminds us that rain does not fall on one man's house alone.

Sorry fe maga dog,
him turn roun bite you

(Hasty acts of charity should be considered.)

Vincent of Bailey's Vale

Vincent could settle an argument with one line of scripture.

Selvin Johnson

Selvin, one of Bob Marley's friends, knew "who colt the game," who knew there was no road so straight, no man so honest as the one that tricked the unwary.

Who colt the game?

(Who made deliberate wrong moves to change the outcome of the plan?)

Wan-wan coco full basket

(Wealth can be accumulated a little at a time.)

Dreamy Leroy Harrow

Dreamy built his house one board at a time. He used to say, "One shouldn't go without while another goes with." Dreamy is generous.

16

Hear

In that day the Lord shall take away the bravery of their
tinkling ornaments about their feet, and their cauls,
and their round tires like the moon,
The chains, and the bracelets and the mufflers,
The bonnets, and the ornaments of the legs, and the
headbands, and the tablets, and the earrings,
The rings, and nose jewels,
The changeable suits of apparel, and the mantles, and the
wimples, and the crisping pins,
The glasses and the fine linen, and the hoods, and the
veils.

ISAIAH 3:18–23

Our little school in the hills of St. Mary was not an easy thing to run, and this summer the rains came early and the rivers filled with drowned chickens; and this summer the students learned to eat fish cheeks, a delicacy in Jamaica but in America, another story. Another time there was a great drought, and our water tank was dry and we had to bribe the water commission trucker for water. He was a Rastaman and would not fill a tank if he did not like you. Many was the night I reasoned with him on the top of the hill above the school. In the end, after many reasonings and not a small number of Red Stripe beers, our Redeemer deposited fresh parish water into our tank and the students no longer had to carry water buckets from the sea to flush toilets in their dorm rooms.

This is the stuff that makes people "walk good" as they say in Jamaica and makes you thankful for that flick of the wrist that sends the water rushing, flushing. Afterward some of us still bathe in the sea but the freedom from hauling buckets is a real reprieve; and a glass of water has a whole new meaning for many.

I remember doing our laundry down by the river and the women singing and scrubbing shirts and pants on river rocks and the bamboos bowing and clicking musically in the breeze and the wet clothes, spread out on stones in the sun to dry, and later smelling like the many rivers that empty into the sea and all of it somehow summed-up in the Jamaican saying, "River stone settle deep don't feel hot sun up top." Or as we also say in America, you don't miss your water until your well runs dry. Or the man who has everything knows nothing. Or perhaps the idea that one person not feeling any pain doesn't know the anguish of those who do. One expression—so many applications.

We spend all day Friday at the outdoor market in Port Maria buying vegetables and fruit. My wife Lorry and I do much of the marketing with Mackie who shows us the tricks of the trade. Mainly this consists of how to bargain, how to spot good from bad, fresh from going and gone. The other thing he teaches is how to reason with a seller and make a deal that is satisfactory for everyone.

The market is close to the grayish, lichen-encrusted Anglican church behind which the ocean is either rambunctious or flat-blue. Canopied, open-aired, the market is a cacophony of sound. Men laughing, grunting, reasoning while toting huge sacks of yams. Women bawling—"Chocho, mango, come touch me tomato!" Goats, large and little, wandering daintily outside the compound among kids with sticks training a wheel to roll.

The smells are horrific to some of our students. Too strong, too full of tropic vitriol and rot; the queer metal smell of blood, ripe sewage, and the sea water sloshing in a putrid narrow canal ditch. This rottenness mixed with the fresh fragrance of produce straight from the farm—all these odors are more than some Americans can take. I watch one student after another abandon ship and fade into the shade.

Mackie haggles with the best of the higglers, his loud Scottish brogue laugh, "Ahhhh" telling when everything is right and his blank iron-edge silence when it is not, and then the soft, almost dangerous-sounding, "No, mon," when an argument is about to break out. As soon as the deal is consummated and the folded bills have sprouted out of the hands of the higglers—they pack them between their fingers—I grab up a scratchy burlap sack of yellow yam, white yam, and carry it out to the over-weighted Morris vehicle, then back for more sacks of corn (in Jamaica, cows, not people feed on this, but we like the way it tastes) and scandal bags jammed with carrots, thyme, onions, garlic, cassava, melons, cucumbers, soursop, sweetsop, julie mangos, black mangos, otaheite apples, pawpaw, and pumpkins, all carried and stowed into the trunk of the rental car whose springs sink lower and lower until the back bumper is almost touching the road. If we hit a pothole, the day could take a different turn.

The sweat runs in little rivers off me but Mackie's face gleams like polished black coral. He is a small man but he can tote anything on his shoulders or his head. The higglers at this great booming food circus respect Mackie the same way I do. He is a master of tact and righteous-ness, a savvy, sensible complex individual who moves among people as if he were born to lead them out of despair. I ask him, "Is there anything you can't do?" And he answers, "No, mon." He can easily fix electricity, plumbing, heal a swollen lip with bissy nut or a rash with cerasee, run or swim miles, smoke a pound of herb, reason with Bob Marley's ital cook, or write a reggae song. He can bargain and butt heads with the best of them. He can laugh. He can dance.

The heat comes in waves. A living stew of body odor, life, and death and free-for-all tongue lashing and then at noon the rain comes pounding the zinc roof of the marketplace, and it sounds like a thousand iron drums. So much noise, so much sweat and confusion that, for the moment, the earth seems to be rolling like a breaching whale. I feel I am at sea, feel I am drowning in mother nature's splendor and humanity's squalor and my knees start to wobble and my eyes begin to blur. "It's the heat," I tell myself. To prove I'm okay, I bend down to get a sack of melons. The blood rushes to my head, daylight dims, fades. I hear the sounds of the market but my vision is shrouded in darkness. What is this?

I sink into a Jamaican squat.

There's a loud tearing sound behind me—right behind me.

And a feeling of air conditioning.

I stand up, thinking I might run out of there.

My eyesight returns, I realize my little faint has passed.

But looking down, I see my pants are torn up the back and the front, dividing the material into halves, open at the crotch in front and back, and, to make matters worse, I am wearing red, gold and green undershorts—Rasta shorts, silky and shiny, a present from my wife.

The market—or most of it anyway—is suddenly quiet.

Even the torrential rain lets up, and as if for theatrical display, the sun shines.

There's this dripping, and sun shining, then . . . and then it comes. Laughter so loud it makes donkeys bray. Laughter so convulsive it drowns out the sea.

The entire market is roaring!

I'm standing still—I've no idea what to do.

I quickly look at Mackie—he's laughing with the rest of them. And when he sees my face, he doubles up, gagging for air. Mackie, normally so Scotch-Scotch serious, slapping his thigh, roaring.

My shorts are not just Rasta, by the way, they're the national colors of Jamaica. There I stand, skin to the wind, the laughing wind tickling me, reminding me I'm just a monkey in disguise for the saying is: "the higher the monkey goes, the more he does expose."

Remembering that I am somehow healed of embarrassment, and

with nothing else to do, or be done, I haul off the melons with the breeze blowing through my legs, and I stow them in the 1960s Morris rental car, and go back for more sacks. One bag after another, Mackie and I load up the tiny car until there is no room for anything but a driver, and then Lorry and I squeeze in, sit atop the yams, and Mackie drives up the road to Blue Harbour.

Although nothing more is said about my big moment at market, after I change into another pair of pants, my ripped pair mysteriously disappears. Without my knowing it, Pansy, Blue Harbour's housekeeper, has sent the pants by bicycle boy over to Race Course. There, Miss Icy, the village seamstress, has expertly stitched them together and pressed them too.

And shortly before dinner, I put the offending pants back on.

We have a great meal of stew peas with spinners, little dumplings of tight, twisted dough. There's hard dough bread too, one of the most delicious, dense, starchy breads on earth.

At school, we have a nightly ritual of reading aloud from our journals, after which, the croaker lizards begin their thematic night call and the ratbats begin to waken and yawn and the "bat" moths come around the yard as do the blinkies, the fireflies of the salt-sweet night.

I'm still feeling funny, maybe a little light-headed from market day. I take a walk by myself along the Maypan coconut walk, no more than a narrow goat trail that leads to the village of Castle Gordon. Lances of moonlight cut through the silver-trunked silence of the bush, the only sound being palm fronds scraping the ground with their claws and the scuttling of large black land crabs that the East Indians of this island love to boil and eat.

I sit by the small trickling spring and lean against the nearest palm marveling at how tight and well my pants fit—just like new!

Under the darkest almond trees behind the spring, I hear what sounds like a stifled sob. There is a herd of goats in the maypans and I imagine that's what it is.

Then comes a keening sound. No goat would do that.

Who's there? I call.

The leaves rustle. Nothing.

Then a disembodied voice, "Please, don't leave me."

"Who's there?" I demand.

"Me," utters a tiny voice.

"Who are you?"

"Me."

My eyes scan the pewtered leaves trying to see the figure that might be there, but whoever it is doesn't want to be seen, so I stand up, turn around and start walking toward the moonlit sea.

"Nuh leave, mon, me beg you."

I turn again. "What do you want?"

A shadow floats out of the night.

An almond, borne by the wind, hurtles down and strikes the earth.

Same time, the voice of a man standing pale in the moon says, "Me try hard fe get a work. Me try hard, mon. But there no work for the righteous. Only for the wicked dem."

I listen to the sea roll pebbles in the surf. The man comes a little closer. He is about my size but I can't see him distinctly since he is in almond shadow. "Me haffa good heart. Me haffa good intention." This was followed by a short silence, then: "Why must me try so hard fe find a work? Why must me turn fool? Why must me fret and fret so? Must me murder up and down? Must me die fe nothing?"

I am wondering what to say when the man comes up to me.

In the moonglow, his skin is greyish blue. He's got no shoes, no shirt or pants, he is standing in his underpants, and as the moon momentarily slides behind a cloud, it's as if a pair of underpants is talking to me: "Me have no pant, me have no shirt, me have no shoe. Me have just what you see me wear, me own skin and these pitiful likkle short."

"What is it you want?"

"Me haff no money."

"I understand that."

"You don't."

"We all have troubles, mon."

"No, mon. You don't know what troubles is."

"What, then?"

"You don't know nothing."

I am silent and then I have an idea.

I slip out of my pants and give them to the man.

Then I take off my shirt, and give him that too.

Around my waist is the money belt I take to market. It is full of low-denomination bills, what Jamaicans call *smalls*. I give him a handful and it feels like a lot but it's probably not more than twenty U.S. dollars.

"That's what I have," I tell the man.

I look at him standing half in moonlight, half in shadow.

I feel the wind on my bare skin for the second time today.

The man puts on the sewn pants and the clean shirt and fades into the almond leaves. I do not believe I will ever see him again—if, in fact, I saw him at all. In truth, I heard him. But I did not really see him. I felt him. As I felt my own loss of self that day. I'd felt naked since noon, since the rip of pride reduced me to my essential self, let's say. There is a Rasta expression—help the weak if you are strong. But I don't feel strong or weak, this night, standing in the moon, alone, listening to what might or might not be my own footfalls on the almond leaves.

Next morning, Julie, the cook says, "Someone leave you fish."

There is a fresh-caught parrot fish lying on a banana leaf on the kitchen counter.

"Who left this?" I ask Julie.

"Mon from the village."

"What did he look like?"

She smiles. "Him look like . . . a mon."

17

Obeah

Thou shalt not make unto thee any graven image, or any
likeness of any thing that is in heaven above, or that
is in the earth beneath, or that is in the water under
the earth:
Thou shalt not bow down thyself, nor serve them . . .

EXODUS 20:4–5

The origin of the word *obeah* is cast in obscurity. Some scholars believe it comes from the West African word *obayi,* which means sorcerer. There are male and female practitioners of obeah in Jamaica and its link to Haitian voodoo or vaudaux is known—as is its practical focus—its familiar uses in society. For instance, obeah practitioners may preside over births, deaths, daily investments, house and land disputes. Obeah is often used when good luck and ritual blessing are in short supply, and the obeah man or woman sometimes acts as marriage counselor, love potion activator, and psychologist.

While gathering material for this book, my wife and I visited an obeah man whose name was Sweet Pea, a short, fat man whose office was in back of a bar tended by his wife.

To meet Sweet Pea, we first had to meet his wife, and it was she who decided if we were "worthy"—that is, if we had any money. When after a beer and chat, she decided we were valid clients, she ushered us to her husband's door.

There was a long queue of people stretched out under the almond trees. Some were well dressed, others were not. All had faces of despair, anticipation, or grief. Sweet Pea's wife introduced us to her husband by saying we were "on important business," and he should let us go in immediately, which he did.

We sat at a lace-covered table. The walls of the small room were laden with plastic, fired clay, and porcelain icons. Pets, saints, Virgin Mary, and Jesus sat shelved in a spacious cabinet with comic-strip characters and action heroes like Batman and Robin, the Flash, Aquaman, Godzilla, Bullwinkle Moose, Daffy Duck, Smoky the Bear, and myriad others gilded and gleaming, silvered and shining. These were used for ceremonial purposes, to bless or curse someone, to call upon as spiritual advisor or helper or conduit to another world of succor and obeisance.

We understood that a contemporary obeah man, especially a good one—and Sweet Pea was quite good—is a necromancer, magician, psychic, occult doctor, and hands-on practitioner. He is a man of herbal remedy and a dispenser of medicine. His methods and manners were his own, and each obeah man has a certain style: one rides upon a white horse in a secret pasture and conducts ceremonies at eventide; another, like Sweet Pea sits like a magistrate in his mad gallery of iconography. His fat fingers are ringed in gold and diamonds because, as we have heard, the people of St. Mary have made this man rich as a king. Rastas are fond of saying, "He dines on the blood of the people and is a draculizer."

Sweet Pea's way is to listen to a patient and then to offer a cure.

What could Sweet Pea do for us?

Anything from securing a lost passport to damaging the eyesight of an enemy, or taking out any opposition in our life: this he states with assurance and solemnity.

It is a fact that obeah men sometimes use their power to take out their own competition—in other words—they will sometimes wipe out another obeah man. If this sounds like the darker aspect of television drama voodoo, it's because it is, in fact, like that.

The obeah man is a priest of polarity, a deacon of divisiveness, but he is also a man of great common sense who can always smell a rat. His manner of household healing may be complex or quite simple. He may spray you with hundred-proof white rum: that is, spit it on you. Or he may tell you to burn a certain number of arcane leaves in an urn. Thus your son might awaken and seek an institution of higher learning; thus an actual rat, a rodent, might pack up and leave your kitchen.

After chatting with us for a while, Sweet Pea asks, "What do you want to know?" His eyes are large and scrutinous, as if he could see right through our skin.

I say, "I would like to know the owner of this ring."

I hold up a small gold ring.

Sweet Pea takes it in his glittery hand. He studies it. He closes his fist over it and shakes it around like a pair of dice. Then he says in a stentorian Roman orator's voice: "I now invoke all the saints that watch over us . . ." and he proceeds to name them, one after another.

The saints had familiar names like Saint Michael and Saint Bartholomew but also peculiar ones like Saint Garbagio, Saint Aloysius Ribbentrop, Saint Tony, and Saint George the Gorgeous.

Sweet Pea piles on the names of fabulous and irregular saints, who work for him and come at his bidding, and you can feel them piling on as if they were spiritual linebackers at a football game of the gods.

Then with a small flourish of hands—rubbing both of them together very vigorously—Sweet Pea's litany ends with Saint-Joe-From-Puerto-Rico-With-Beard, and he tosses the ring into a glass of water.

Surprisingly, the ring sinks lazily to the bottom of the glass.

"What kind of water is that?" my wife asks.

"Spring water," Sweet Pea replies.

"Any particular kind?"

He eyes her cannily, then answers, "That which is the domicile of a certain mermaid."

Sweet Pea's expression hardens, he smiles at Lorry indulgently. "Now, please," he says, focusing on me, "Mention a number of names, any names at all, and when you get to the owner of the ring, which of course I should know nothing of, something will happen."

"What might that be?" I ask.

"That is for the ring to say." Then he adds, "Alpha and Omega, Enoch as the seventh from Adam, bear witness now as the sea and raging waters foam in shame and as wandering stars are born from blackness of darkness and as the ten thousand saints murmur their myrmidons and swell to oratatives: *okaheeghan in dominae exeuntae provisorath cum mockitude,* now, I command you, set forth the vigilance of eternal fire and free the captive name!"

And the gold ring starts rattling in the glass of water; then it settles and is still.

Nothing happens.

Sweet Pea sighs, scratches his nose, snorts.

"Did you mention the correct owner of the ring?" he demands.

I admit, "I got carried away with all the names and the recitation."

"And you didn't include the one name?"

"I didn't."

He regards me as the father regards the forgetful son. "Now if you would do it again," he says softly, chidingly, "and this time, remember to include the owner of the ring with all of the others, but do not change the tone of your voice, say the names all in the same matter-of-fact way. Is that understood? Say them all the same."

I nod and do this thing, and I pay no attention to his mumbling in tongues and when I say, "Bill" (who is the owner of the ring), the ring begins to vibrate and then, miraculously, it rises to the top of the glass and floats for a moment, and then slowly sinks.

"It is this Bill who owns the ring?" Sweet Pea asks. It is a question but the voice is unquestioning.

"Yes, it belongs to our friend, Bill, who is staying at Blue Harbour."

Sweet Pea smiles.

For the first time I see that his teeth are gold.

He then nods toward the door and mentions that many are called and few are chosen. His fee? 750 dollars JA (100 U.S. dollars).

And all for a magic trick that none of us can figure out.

Mackie had refused to come into the yard, but now, behind the wheel, he laughs when we tell him what happened. "Obeah men are devils," he says. "You won't find no Rasta to enter that false man's temple."

Driving through Port Maria, the streets bright and loud and full of unknown smells, some good, some bad, some awful, Mackie tells us in his deep voice, "You must purify the ill effects of that man. You may think him a show, but him dangerous."

That night Mackie sets a leaf from a leaf of life plant in our bedroom. Then he and Roy blow ganja smoke in the four corners, and Mackie reads from the Bible about how Solomon refused the tablets of idolatry and crushed the golden figures of insect gods of the Egyptians, and how no graven images are to be worshiped in house or heart or anywhere else.

Mackie tells me, "You dream tonight of red mermaid, wake up quick."

But we do not dream red in our small cedar-floored room presided over by a leaf from the plant of life. We dream of mermaids. Yellow mermaids, green mermaids, blue mermaids, and pink, all of which, in the morning, Mackie says are beneficent because they're the keepers of the springs of life just like the plant guardian that watched over us while the tribes of stars wheel over our heads.

But, he adds, just to be sure Sweet Pea's spirit-saints aren't snooping around the premises, a prescription of sanctity was necessary—an all-day reading from Isaiah, chapters 3 to 7—which is all about the fire devouring the stubble, and the flame consuming the chaff, and the Lord of Hosts casting out the unclean, and the roaring, oh, yes, the roaring of the lions.

I ask who Sweet Pea's spirit-saints are.

Mackie answers, "Some of them are men he killed."

18

Believers

*For as yet they knew not the scripture, that he must rise
again from the dead.*

JOHN 20:9

Raggy, son of Jango and Geddy and brother of Son, is a one-of-a-
kind old-time believer. Rootsman, not locksman, Raggy is a rootical
back country, freewheeling East Indian Jamaican whose friends are
Rasta. But he holds to no singular faith that you could name. There
are so many like this in the Parish of St. Mary and in the hills of
St. Ann.

One time when I asked Raggy where he fit into the picture, faith-
wise, so to say, he squinted at me, gave me one of his crinkle-eye, cackle
laughs, saying, "Me no know." When I pressed him further, he said,
"I'm a natural mystic. You see, I smoke the sacrament but don't wear
the lock. I have no lock on my head or my heart. I just live an I-life."
Countryman, the Jamaican actor, who is also an East Indian Jamaican,
once said the same thing to me: "I-life."

Raggy is hard to describe. He can fix a toaster or a carburetor in
minutes. He can repair a computer. He can swim miles out in the
open ocean. He is afraid of nothing and in love with everything. He
once told me that if you want to know when a hurricane is coming,

"Look at the fowl when they perch in a tree. If you want to know how bad the hurricane going to be, check how high the fowl roost."

Lately he has been instructing me in the ways of Obeah. Raggy is small, yet powerful and very quick on his feet. If anyone favored the mongoose, it was Raggy with his cunning, crinkling eyes, his captivating, missing-tooth smile, and his cackly, catchy laugh.

Raggy has super-abundant mystical powers. He can spirit a guinep off a tall tree by looking at it a certain way. He can get you to loan him money without asking. He can also loan you money if you need it, but he never seems to have any money on him; like the guinep, Raggy's money is on a money tree somewhere in the bush of ghosts. He drives cars that seem to have come from an automobile museum.

I had the pleasure of driving one of his piecemeal specials called "the Cockroach" because, in Jamaica, cockroaches never die.

This unkillable Cockroach is a patchwork, sheet metal, banged-together putty-puss vehicle made from a few hundred others. The frame might be Toyota but the rest of it is untraceable. The wipers are handmade. They whack the windshield good but they don't move water one way or another. The day I drive the Cockroach, it is a deadly downpour all the way to Montego Bay, a drive of about a hundred miles from Castle Gordon, and every time I hit a pothole (of which there were a few thousand) I felt it up my back teeth and down to the roots of my hair.

Raggy, short for Raggamuffin, cleans his nails with a ratchet knife. Some say he files his teeth, but those are his enemies talking. Raggy has lots of enemies especially up in Mason Hall where a local obeah man has put out a warrant on Raggy's soul.

As one of Raggy's oldest friends, I seldom beg him a *bli,* which means, in Jamaica talk, I don't ask him for *favors.* Instead I just ask him to help me out, and he always does.

I spend hours talking to Raggy about the supernatural: mainly duppies. A couple days ago, he said, "You know, late at night sometime me hear some likkle small noise inside the main house. I know this is a duppy, so I don't go in there fe trouble."

"You ever see Noel Coward's ghost?"*

"Not as yet. But me *hear* his duppy all the while."

"Why is he still here, I wonder? I mean, why didn't he just skip the in-between world and go straight to heaven?"

Raggy thinks this is funny. He starts laughing, jackknifing at the knees, laughing so hard he is not laughing anymore, he is just making the face of a laughing man and expelling air, but no sound is coming out. Then he catches my shoulder and says in his soft, hoarse voice, "Gerry mon, Duppy don't need no reason to do what him do. Duppy do what him *want* fe do."

Just then Roy comes into the conversation. He is standing next to me and he says, "Dem people do a whole lot of wickedness back in dem time. Dem naked, ya know. Dem travel 'bout wid a towel or dem just go naked, and me seh, me no know what dem do. Dem wicked, mon."

This of course is the Rasta view and I might add, as I've heard it many times before, extremely homophobic and recriminatory but quite old-school Rasta, the Biblical fear of sodomy of any kind, of spilling the sacred seed of life.

Coward and company, their Babylonian ways, their Sodom and Gomorran secret customs, their rampant hedonism, colonialism, what the Rastas call "dem old, old pirate mentality": these things are as necessary to avoid as eating shellfish, pork, and consuming salt, and for some, even using Babylon utensils such as machine-made knives and forks. The really strict Rastas use gourds for eating bowls and hand-carved utensils.

I've heard it again and again, the Rasta view that Coward and company were bad men, but I can never get anyone holding this opinion to tell me what Mr. Coward did that was wrong except that he was gay.

---

*British playwright Noel Coward (1899–1973) came to Jamaica in the late 1940s as a guest of Ian Fleming, author of the James Bond novels. Coward built two residences in St. Mary, including our school site, Blue Harbour, and later, Firefly, situated 1,200 feet above Blue Harbour. He lived there, off and on, until 1973 when he passed peacefully at Firefly. Many people have seen his spirit, or duppy, including ourselves and many of our students.

"That is no crime," I say. "It's an attitude, a preference, a predisposition that circuits through the DNA of a human being. One can't, or shouldn't, place judgment upon it," I tell them. But they do.

"Well," Roy admonishes. "You want fe know why dem round de place? You want fe know why dem keep return from de dead?"

"Tell me."

"Dem nuh peaceful, mon. Dem travel de earth lookin' for peace but dem nuh find-i'. Dem sit down by the rivers of water but dem no have nuh song fe sing, an no drink fe soothe dem troat. Dem weep fe dere own wickedness. Dem live *unnatural*. Dem die unnatural. Dem live as a dead: unnatural." This is very nearly the mythic rationale of the undead vampire, I think.

Roy flashes and flails his dreadlocks to underscore, or rather, as he says, overscore, his argument, his anti-gay point of view.

Raggy, sitting on the back porch steps, head cradled in his right hand, elbow on knee, chuckles at Roy's inveterate passion. He doesn't have so rigid a view about anything. He thinks the world is a funny place to be. He waits for the next thing to laugh at. "Duppy don't need fe travel all bout de yard, you know. Him dream yuh wherever him at; him mek we do de walkin' and frettin'; and what him do? Him do nuttin'. So it go."

Morris, our night watchman, enters into the conversation. Morris is an older man. Rootical, they say, rather than Rasta. But Morris is very wise in the world of proverbs. He knows Solomonic sayings and he knows the Bible. He is African and French with a face of teak. Long ago Morris's family emigrated from the island of Martinique where voodoo was, and still is, a practice among many. I've heard Rastas say disparagingly that Morris practices his own diabolism, whatever it might be, perhaps nothing other than rumor but maybe a very subtle brand of obeah. Nonetheless, I find him to be a mystic man, one who like Raggy keeps it all on the sly, and also like Raggy, lives well apart from the people. Raggy now lives on Firefly Hill in a stone and mortar kind of wattle-and-daub one-room cottage with a dirt floor. Morris lives in one room of an abandoned and crumbling mansion. Both men live on the edge of a cliff.

Raggy tells me he knows the sorcerer of Mason Hall and empha-
sizes that this wicked man is still after him and his family. Using magic,
this obeah man burned Raggy's family's house to the ground—sponta-
neous combustion—it might be called. In some places on the island,
they would say *fireballs*.

Roy has done battle with obeah himself. He was once attacked by
a crab duppy and then again by a dog duppy: both spirits of the dead
directed to do evil deeds by an obeah man. Roy defeated them, he says,
using the oaths and powers of lionhood: spiritual Rastafarian karate.
"No hand moves, but a deadly hand strikes." Bob Marley spoke of being
a "Duppy Conqueror." "The bars could not hold me/Force could not
control me now."

Bull buckra—bullies—cannot hold down the good man who knows
the Most High is on his side.

According to some local myths, Morris delves into the dark arts whenever he needs to, but most often, when he himself is attacked by something supernatural. People in the village of Castle Gordon swear that
Morris has alchemized and delivered dangerous potions. People say he
has cast curses, disposed of enemies, made invisible barriers all around
his sequestered living quarters. They say you have only to look into
Morris's eyes to know the power he possesses. So people say . . .

I have always thought Morris was a brethren. He is sort of ageless
in face and form—wrinkleless—a man of perfect posture. He could be
in his late sixties, as some say. But I don't think he looks a day over
thirty-five. On a moonless night, Morris's skin is so dark, your eye can't
pry him away from a shadow. He is virtually invisible, which is precisely
why he is such a superior night watchman.

"Have you seen the duppies of Blue Harbour?" I ask him.

Morris smiles vaguely, his eyes sparkling yet always searching.
"Certainly," he says, nodding many times. "I have seen him, and his
friends, too." Morris speaks proper English, rarely patois, unless he is
enjoying a drink at a local bar, and then the patois springs forth unbidden and natural.

I ask him, "What did Mr. Coward look like?"

"Like a man. Like Tom or Bill, or anyone you know."

"A man of flesh, in other words."

"That is what we are taught, what we learn. That is what we *see* with our eyes."

"So you've *seen* Noel Coward walking around?"

"His life is not done, mon. No, sir. You see, Coward's life is still going on. Because life, no matter how you cut it, burn it, or tear it apart, life itself must rule, life itself must live. That is the law we know."

"Even dead?"

"Just so. Look, here, now. This is my hand. Does my hand know what my mind is thinking? By itself, it is merely a hand. If I cut it off my arm, will it walk away? You may say, no, but yet that hand has some spirit of its own, some mind of its own. And if a man cleverly schooled in the arts you mentioned—obeah or voodoo or whatever—wants that hand to perform, for *him,* well, that is just what *him* going to do: and the hand obey. Yes, sir. That hand obey."

The discussion ends on that note, as Roy has bananas to harvest on the plantation, and Raggy's got a boat engine to fix, and Morris is on his way to hunt a yellow boa that ate one of his chickens. So he goes off with a well-sharp machete.

In fact, all three men have a well-sharp machete. "Third arm," they call it here.

Two days later, however, this very same conversation is picked up at the Blue Harbour Bar. When Jamaicans say, "Soon come," they mean any time soon: an hour, a day, a week, or a month. When they say to each other, "See you in time," the reply to this is always, "More time."

I sit at the bar as Raggy is saying, "Listen me, now. A dead haffa reason fe come back. Him dream you, mon, cause im need you fe find his treasure."

"What treasure?" I ask.

"Well," Raggy says, "Mr. Coward is a man that do lots of likkle thing that mek him money, seen?"

"So you think there is a treasure of some kind buried away at Blue Harbour?"

"Some likkle ting worth a whole heap of money, an him want you fe find-i'." His eyes crinkle, he chuckles.

I will play this game and see where it goes. "So what do we look for, Raggy?"

Julie comes over with a platter of fried plantain, boiled eggs, calaloo, sliced pineapple, and pawpaw.

Soon we are all munching, and Raggy continues with his riches theme while sipping hot Tetley tea with much condensed sweet milk. I say, "Since Noel Coward was a writer, what would he hide away at Blue Harbour—a play?" That has actually been my thought for some time, that there were literary archives stored away somewhere in the upstairs back bedroom that was once an office.

Raggy whistles through his teeth. "Any ting, mon. Any likkle ting."

I nod.

"Look fe them," Raggy adds, sipping his Tetley.

"Where?"

Raggy points to Villa Rose nestled in a copse of ruby bougainvillea blossoms. "A secret play script," Lorry remarks, as she passes by with some guava punch. "How interesting."

Raggy finishes his tea. "Him a painter?"

"Quite a good one."

"Him painting worth money then?"

"Lots of money—at auction," Lorry mentions.

Raggy studies Villa Rose. The red zinc roof is hot pink in the white morning sun. "That where him work," Raggy muses. "Tonight, mek we try fe see where him hide his thing." Then he brushes knuckles with me and goes off, saying, "Me gotta fix Mike cyar. Soon come."

After breakfast, with the help of some of our students, Lorry and I search the library. There is nothing of great interest there, but we find a small trunk full of signed first editions in the laundry room. Books by all manner of famous people from royals to rebels, and then there are some James Bond novels signed by Ian Fleming to Sir Noel.

The man knew everyone from Somerset Maugham to Lawrence of Arabia.

More is the pity, as Noel might say, that all of these fine old antiquarian books are being eaten by silverfish. But I sincerely doubt that people will stop seeing his ghost if we get his books to a better place.

19

Beast

And I stood upon the sand of the sea, and saw a beast rise
out of the sea . . .
And the beast which I saw was like unto a leopard, and
his feet were as the feet of a bear, and his mouth as
the mouth of a lion: and the dragon gave him his
power, and his seat, and great authority.

REVELATION 13:1–2

Noel Coward built a swimming pool after a friend showed him a film of a twelve-foot hammerhead shark tearing apart a porpoise in the shallow lagoon at Blue Harbour. This ended the myth that predatory fish couldn't come through the reef. So Coward actually ordered a pool built in the sea itself. It was formed out of coral heads and rocks and concrete was poured on three ends to close it off.

When the pool was finished, there was a pretty little lagoon within the larger one. It admitted the freshening tides but kept the sharks out, and it was (at least for a time) a sandy-bottomed beauty of engineering: an amber pool within a green jade one. Though badly battered by hurricanes of recent years, the old pool isn't so much for swimming as for meditation; a "nice to be alone and listen to the waves booming the windward reef" place.

One day while I am down there listening to the roar of tide and the sound of pebbles rolling in the claws of the breakers, there comes a weird wail from the land side of the pool.

I listen and finally decide the noise comes from a small cavity made by two great boulders that are shouldered up against one another on the south side of the beach.

Walking around these giant rocks, which are large enough to have good-sized saplings on the moss-topped stone, I see the hunched form of a boy crouched in the dappled shade of the giant rocks.

He is sitting against the far end of the natural cave made by the boulders. I see at once that his eyes are milky blue, and his skin is mahogany, shiny, gleaming in the sun. The boy's toes are joined and his feet are webbed. He sings a nasally song that is neither English nor Jamaican patois. After listening for a while, I register a few notes I know from hearing the parishioners of the neo-revival churches in Port Maria. The boy is singing in tongues.

This draws me closer to him, so I can hear him better. But when I come near, he slithers back into the darkest corner of the cave. There, feral and afraid, he cowers.

I speak to him gently.

He stares at me, and the whites of his eyes almost glow in the dark. As my own eyes adjust to the shadows, I notice how strangely shaped the boy's body is. He is more creature than child. More animal than human.

He is now so deep into the cave that I leave him there momentarily and go up hill to find my wife Lorry.

On the way, I remember the old Celtic sulkie legends, the ones about human seals, shape-shifters of the Hebrides.

I find Lorry in the kitchen with our school's cook, Julie. Both want to come down the hill and see the boy. "Him must speak the patois," Julie reassures me. "Me mek him come out into the sun."

Julie's first efforts, however, fall on deaf ears. The boy presses himself, lizardlike, up against the farthest wall of the cave.

Julie coaxes him into the light of day.

The boy cocks his head, listens. Then, gradually withdraws from the socket of darkness, and crawls out on the sand.

In full light I see that he is even more oddly shaped than I imagined. Back bent, arms loopy and long. Standing in front of the cave, he trembles in the sun. His chest is huge, his legs bowed.

But the most amazing thing about him is his feet. They are spatulate—and he has no toes. Feet planted in the red fallen almond leaves, he looks like a crab with his arms pincerlike in front of him, as if he is testing the air with them.

"Him look misbegotten," Julie says with a shake of the head.

"Like him born wid a cowl over him eye," she concludes.

That, in Jamaica talk, means this boy is gifted, or cursed, with a kind of sixth sense, the cowl suggesting that on land his powers are weaker than upon the sea. It also means he is freakishness, most like a pariah kid, homeless or abandoned.

"Bwai," Julie says. The child, despite his preternatural appearance and possible animal prowess, could be anywhere from five to eight.

"Me ask yuh name now," Julie demands.

The boy's eyes wander the headland. Like a trapped animal, he longs for the sea, and his eyes turn in that direction. He doesn't look at Julie, but all around her, and I sense he sees everything peripherally.

He then raises a crooked finger and scribbles on the air. Like an anemone attracting a fish.

"Yuh faddah fisherman?" Julie questions. She drops to one knee, so she is not towering over the boy.

He responds by gazing around at Julie and us suspiciously. I have seen wounded animals do this.

"Yuh hungry, bwai?" Julie presses closer.

For the first time, the child shakes his head.

"Yuh unnerstan' me now, bwai?"

His small round head nods.

Julie sighs. "Weh yuh muddeh now?"

The boy shakes his head, no, looks longingly at the blue sea. He stuffs all the fingers of his right hand into his mouth, as if he intends to eat them. Then he retracts his hand, looks at it, shoves it back in his mouth again and starts sucking on it.

Julie scolds him. "Get yuh hand outta yuh mout when me talk to you, bwai!"

The boy ignores her. His eyes are glued to the sea-wrack, the white waves bashing the reef, the miles of empty ocean, the sun-gleam on sargassum weed.

Julie heaves herself to her feet, says to me, "Him too old fe dat sucking. How old you think him is?"

Lorry says, "Nine or ten."

"Younger," I say.

"Cha!" Julie tosses her head in despair. "Some a dem youth dem grow like chicken. Peck, peck. And dem nyam any old ting—even dem hand." She looks at us and laughs, then says in English, "You know what I mean?"

"They're wild things, the kids of Port Maria," I add.

"Yah, mon. Wild as the wind, with no parent but the sea—and it's she that feed them." Julie grins, half in despair, half in humor. "Well, I get no word outta 'im. Sooner get a rock fe talk. Now I haffa go back to the kitchen and make lunch."

All the while, the big-chest boy with the flat web feet jerks hand from mouth, and wiping it on his torn and ragged swimsuit, says something to Julie's back.

Whatever it is, it sounds like tongues to me, but Julie turns around and places her hands on her hips. The boy hops just like a frog to the ocean's edge, and shouts again to Julie. This time I hear what he says. "Me seh yu favor de mongoose, mon," he squeals.

Julie's mouth drops open. "Yu seh *what*?"

"Me seh yuh favor de mongoose," the boy squeaks.

Then he hops into the sea and stands there uncertainly between shore and shallows, squinting at the snowy white breakers pounding their horse hooves against the coral heads.

"What does he mean by that?" Lorry asks Julie.

Julie guffaws, shakes her head again. "Him se me resemble a mongoose." She throws back her head and says, "Bwai, bwai, me wish me maga like dat fenky-fenky animal."

To us, she adds, "I wish I was skinny as one of them too-lie, too-tief animal." Then she starts up the steep hill toward the house. But on the way she stops once and hollers over the sea roar, "Dat bwai half fish, half-human." She laughs, and leaves. And we are left with the boy, who neither stays nor goes.

A fleecy cloud smudges the sun and a light rain drizzles down.

The whole seaside scene is in shadow.

Suddenly the boy dives into an incoming wave, and disappears.

He surfaces, head all dog slick and shiny, and paddles out toward the reef.

At the same time, a skiff rounds the bend over by Reef Point. There are two people in the skiff, each rain-hunched. A small man and a smaller woman, and they seem to be paddling toward the boy, and the sun struggles free of the fleece and the sun butters the beach with light.

The rain quits.

A rainbow burns brightly over the green thatch of Cabarita Island.

I think—oddly enough—of Dr. Moreau and his crazy island of troglodytes. We believe in stories that beasts come from madness where, in reality, they come from the pressure-cooker of poverty.

"Babylon work, dat," the Rastas say.

I remember my own words from a book published a few years ago: "We fear the wolf because we don't understand the beast within ourselves."

I gaze at the reef as the boy reaches the skiff. The woman drops anchor—the small rusted block of a motor—and then she and her man dive into the crystal sea and the boy squeals and dives with them.

I watch their feet kick in the air before they vanish, and I am not surprised that all six are joined at the toe: feet like flippers passed down the generations, most likely, but who knows.

I sit on a rock and wait for them to surface. The swells chew at the skiff, growl and gnaw it this way and that, nosing it all around.

No heads of divers.

I ask Lorry who's sitting beside me, how long it has been since we last saw them, and she replies, "They've been down for about five minutes."

It seems longer, and when more time elapses, at least another five minutes, I wonder where they went.

The rainbow illuminates the entire sky.

John Crow Mountains, clear of mist for the first time in days, stand out boldly blue-green in the fading light far along the northern coastline. The riderless skiff buck dances in the surf. The blue-white reef combs the key.

The three do not come up again.

We wait another hour.

Then it rains hard and we go up to the house using a banana leaf for a raincoat.

A flock of bright lime-green pocket parrots go cheeping over our heads. We can feel the electricity of their wing beats in our hair.

On the veranda, we throw down our leaf and stare at the bay. Two Jamaican kids use the banana leaf for a water-slider and begin a long, graceful glide across the rain-wet veranda.

The skiff is still there, dark horse tethered to a chunk of cat-iron.

I say to Lorry, "You know the folklore of the sulkies of the British Isles?"

She nods, smiles. "They could bewitch people."

"That boy looked sulkie to me," I say.

The roar of the rain and sawing of the sea drowns me out, yet Lorry smiles, "In the old myths such children were born backward, or like this boy as Julie said, with a cowl, a soft flap of skin like a veil over his eyes. That meant he was born with . . . powers."

"Maybe all three of them were water duppies."

"We fear the beast," she said, and didn't finish.

I think of the Rasta view of the endtimes.

"It doesn't hurt to believe in something," Lorry mentions, reading my mind.

We sit in pandana chairs and listen to the rain drumming on the galvanized roof. Slowly I close my eyes and dream of fish women with sharp, pointed teeth, gold wiry hair, and skin the color of St. Ann honey, and with breasts shapely and full.

The dream fades and I see the scroll of the Seventh Seal unroll underneath the sea and the deep water is loud with mermen and mermaids.

I see beasts with eyes—before and behind—who sing the song of the fallen magister, the desolate angel who is part camel, part man.

Spreeboy, come down from the mountain where he lives, is waiting at the bar for me. I am told he has something important to tell me.

I sip a Dragon stout with him, and Spreeboy says that the time is come when up is down, and the world is no longer the world of man, but the world of beasts, and the days of reckoning are upon us. It is the Rastafarian endtimes conundrum. The word *Sheol* comes and goes and it sounds very real on Spreeboy's lips.

I speak to him of silkies and sulkies, and he nods, sipping his black stout in the darkness, talking low and soft in that dreamy voice of his like sandpaper working a piece of driftwood.

"I saw a strong angel proclaiming with a loud voice, 'Who is worthy to open the book, and to loosen the seals thereof?' And no man in heaven, nor in earth, neither under the earth, was able to open the book, neither to look thereon . . . And one of the elders saith unto me, 'Weep not: behold, the Lion of the Tribe of Judah, the Root of David, hath prevailed to open the book, and to loose the seven seals thereof.'"

So saying, Spreeboy finished his stout and goes out the gate. I watch him as he heads down the road toward the deep fastness of the forest. He turns once and says to me, "Before the throne there was a sea of glass like unto crystal, say His name Rastafari, holy, holy, holy, God Almighty, which was, and is, and is to come. And so say no more."

A small man with a staff made of cedarwood is walking with a one-eyed dog named Brindle that his neighbor tried to kill. A small man with a fearless faith, welcoming the last of days. For it is as he says: "The sorcerers have come again and the nations are deceived. The blood of prophets runs freely in the streets, and the rivers of Babylon run dry."

I watch Spreeboy until he is but a speck in the dark, and then the light that is in him grows dim in the distance and I see only the darkest of nights and hear only the loudest of croaker lizards grating in the guava trees of this incomparable fallen paradise.

20

Switcher

The stranger that is within thee shall get up above thee
very high; and thou shalt come down very low.
He shall lend to thee and thou shalt not lend to him: he
shall be the head and thou shall be the tail.

DEUTERONOMY 28:43–44

I sit up and look around.

I am not at Blue Harbour, our home.

I don't know where I am.

I am not dreaming, but I am not sure I am not dreaming.

I sit on the side of the bed, trying to sort it out.

I am in a huge room, a kind of dormitory. How had I gotten there?

There are lots of beds lined up in neat military rows. I then realize where I am—and better yet—who I am.

Then it strikes me, loud and clear, that . . . I am somebody else.

No, I am myself.

But I am presently stuck in someone else's body.

It is the body of a man who is heavier than I am.

Start with that—I am someone else.

And yet, I do remember my other identity.

So—who am I?

That leads . . . the matter is incalculably complex and confusing . . . to the me within the him.

I manage to stay calm.

I stare at my hands. I lift them up, on command. They rise obediently. I almost expected them not to obey me.

My hands are beautifully dark.

But the fingers are dubiously stubby. I have fingers like cocktail franks.

My fat fingers trip a fabulous memory trove. Hadn't my, well, *former* hands been long and thin like a piano player's?

I'd always sort of liked my hands. These new ones weren't much good to me.

I stuff them into my breast pocket.

They—as if on their own accord—pull out a pack of cigarettes. The fat sausage fingers select a Marlboro, and place it upon my lower lip. My upper lip comes down gently on the filter. Next, the unbidden hand digs into my trouser pocket and produces a small box of wooden matches. Now I am smoking. But I am not and never was a smoker.

Now I was. Or, I mean, am.

And I was, or actually am, enjoying each inhalation, each long, satisfying exhalation.

Smoking, I am fully in the present tense.

Myself upon the earth, smoking.

All right. It is not my body I am ruining.

Or is it? You see what I mean . . . inescapably confusing.

The question arises: Why, at some other time and in some other body, didn't I like smoking? And why do I like it now? If only I could figure that out . . .

It comes to me when I see my feet.

These are plump and fatuous feet, unattractive, unathletic-looking, and while (it comes to me in a flash) I once had nice feet and runner's calves, strong and muscled from years of long-distance running, and there it was—the answer to my question(s) . . .

I don't like smoking because I am an athlete of some kind, which is to say, I was such. But, obviously—with this fatty-fatty butt and big chunk legs, thighs like hams, fingers of pork—I wasn't in the mood for running anymore. Smoking, yes, running, no.

Some other "personal" things, that is, from my other self, come to me now.

In another life, I was, or maybe still am, a teacher.

I have a wife and two children. I work at a school!

I work at a summer school.

In Jamaica.

There it is—the whole ball of wax.

The summer school comes into focus like a snapshot in my brain. The main building is blue. Well, not exactly blue, all over, but mostly blue.

Blue, blue, blue . . .

Harbour. Put together.

Blue Harbour.

Yes, that is the school.

I teach at Blue Harbour, and there, in my alternative life, I am happily married, or so I now believe.

Now—where the hell am I?

I have a good look at my hands, my arms, my body, in general.

Okay then. I am a real live black man whereas before, I am quite sure I was white, or something of that sort. Maybe white and something else.

I can accept the bulk of my body, the hue of my skin—but where is it? Where am I?

This is the scary part. I must also accept that I am wearing a custodial uniform of some sort: white pants, white shirt.

I am sitting on a bed in a long dormitory-like room with lots of other beds.

There are many bodies in the beds. Presumably asleep. Dark bodies.

Dark of face, hand, and foot. Definitely not dead, for I can see them breathing.

The sheets on the beds are white. The bodies, partially covered, are in stark contrast to the sheets.

There is an open window in front of me. I stand up softly in my bare, fat feet and look out into the empty night.

It's quiet out there. I can readily see that the building I am in is made of gray stone, no, white-washed stone. Directly below the window is a parking lot, a couple cars in it.

One of the cars is burned, all rusted-out, and full of bullet holes.

This causes me a moment of wonder.

Bullet holes?

I think to myself: those who run up against the law are punished. The burned and shot-up car has been punished.

Have I been punished?

Is that why I am here?

As well as the sleepers all around me?

I hear them now, and it is as if my ears suddenly clear, as if I have been deep diving and my ears pop and open, and now I can hear clearly.

The other men, all dark, are snoring, breathing, turning and creaking, and making noises with their mouths, tongues, lips.

It comes to me now that this heavy body of mine has done wrong.

I am being punished.

All this passes in the time it takes me to—ow!—smoke a cigarette down to the filter and burn myself.

I pitch the cigarette out the open window and sit on the bed.

I fish out another cigarette.

Why not? It's not my body, why should I care.

My right arm itches. I scratch it absently while I smoke.

The itch worsens. I look at my arm.

On my right forearm there is a burn that runs all the way up to my shoulder. The skin is smooth there. I trace the burn-run with my index finger.

Suddenly, I feel tears wet my face, my cheeks.

I wipe the tears from my eyes. A bell rings. I shudder with fear. A lot of the men, who are dressed like me, leap from their beds. There must be a hundred or more, all black, all punished.

They do not seem as alert as I am. They are stretching and yawning. I am the only one smoking.

I hear a hard-edged voice say, "Come away from that window." I realize I am standing again by the window, and smoking.

"Put that cigarette out!"

I pitch the cigarette out the window, the ember arcing in the darkness.

There is a shuffle of moving, messing, mixing men, all talking in low conversant tones. In the pandemonium, I am unsure which bed is mine. I have a headache. My eyes are not seeing very well. Everything is starting to get hazy. People are talking but I can't hear them very well, and my ears are plugging as if I am slipping under the surface of things . . .

I hear a cock crow.

I am walking out of the place into the night. No one seems to see me leave. I walk outside into the summery night and disappear into the gloom of the coconut grove across the road.

I can hear the sea, I can smell the moonlight on the palms and the scent of damp earth, and I can walk freely, here and there, and it doesn't matter what direction I am going because the night, the darkness, the stillness take care of everything.

> *I am invisible.*
> *The sun is on the rise.*
> *The wind is up.*
> *I smell the salt of the sea.*
> *Tears well up in the corners of my eyes.*
> *I see my appointed place—a rock by the sea under*
>   *the coconut palms.*

A thin man comes down to me from the road.
"I need my body back," he says.
I recognize him. He is me.
I am not me; I am still him, fat and stumpy.
It's idiotic, but perfectly true.
The exchange happens quickly, I barely notice.
The souls move first, switch-bitch, like a light going on,
*   and one going off. Just like that, no different.*
There's a different hum in me now.
I am sitting on the rock and the sun is coming up, and
*   he, my switcher, is walking up through the almond*
*   trees toward Highgate.*
I can see his fat butt pumping up and down.
My hands are my own, my legs feel long and strong.
I think I will run back to Blue Harbour in the dawn.

The following day everything was quite normal. Mackie and I went to Highgate to get supplies for the school. Highgate is the small mountain village where the son of Oliver Cromwell was exiled. After my experience of the night before, I somehow imagined that I knew how Richard Cromwell, Lord Protector of England in 1658, felt. To be transported to the jungle highlands of Jamaica. To be exiled for twenty years. To awaken in the Jamaican dreamtime, a man of power and ambition, thwarted. I imagined eighteenth-century Cromwell striding the wind-bent hills of Highgate, wondering if he would ever waken into the man he once was. Wondering if he would waken as I had into himself.

Buying bammy, potatoes, and rice at Haber's Market, I found the disparity of my situation laughable. I was seeing into things of the spirit that I'd never known before. I was waking into the dreamtime and finding that I had been there before, that my selves were scattered like dry leaves, that I was not one but many. Over a bushel of Irish potatoes, I told Mackie about my dream. He smiled once, then: "Come, mon, mek we show you the place you dream about, me show you the mon, if him alive."

After we paid our bill and stored the boxes of groceries in the back of our rental van, Mackie drove over the hill a few miles to the town of Richmond, another small, timeless Jamaican village. At one end of the town the road ended at a cul-de-sac. In front of us was a large, white, institutional building. It looked like a hospital or a prison. Mackie said it was the latter. "Recognize this place?" he asked, lighting a cigarette and rolling down the window of the van. I nodded; it was my dream with daylight on it.

Mackie put the van in gear and drove close to the stone gate. On the right side of the gate, just inside the compound, I noticed the burnt shell of a Lada, a Russian automobile, riddled with bullet holes and covered with rust. Now the white building came eerily into focus. Little groups of men wandered about the parking lot, talking and smoking. I saw a chunky man leaning out of a second story window smoking a cigarette. He was staring right at me, smiling. I knew him (inside-out). The man kept a steady eye on me, the blue smoke curling from around his mouth. "Where are we, Mackie?"

"Richmond Prison."

"Prison with no bars, no guards?"

"This a first offense prison. Them mon you see there no want fe run way. Them have wife and pickney in town. Them have life here. Them nyam good. Sleep good."

"What happens if they go to a second offense prison?"

"Them don't have it so good there. After this place, them feel like a dead in second offense. Yes, mon. Them do die another death in life."

While we talk the white-shirted and neat-trousered men lounge around the parking lot, smoking and pushing long-handled brooms. Most of them are talking, joking. It doesn't look like a prison; it looks like a country club. My eyes go back to the man in the second story window. I remember now the weight of his bones, the pound of his heart, the grief of his life, the inescapable drudge of it, the fat around his waist, and the scar on his arm.

"I think we should leave now," I tell Mackie. He turns the van around and we drive through the Jamaican countryside.

It is some days later when Mackie explains it to me. His way. In patois. We are in Port Maria buying soft drinks for the students at Foo Hing's warehouse. The heat of the day is hard upon us along with the stink of the garbage-strewn canal that runs in back of the shop. Hefting boxes, I mention to Mackie what I felt when I saw Richmond Prison with him.

Mackie says, "That mon dream you. Him want fe be free. Your spirit was easy pickin' for the right obeah man. Him just pluck you. Same time, you change up."

"Switch identities . . . is that it, then?"

He nods. "It 'appen all de while, mon."

"So, was he . . . in *my* bed while *I* was in *his*?"

"Me don't know."

"But if my spirit was in *his* body, *his* spirit had to be in *my* body."

"Your vibe, mon, all round de place. Not just inna your skin." He laughs.

I hunt around in my head for the right myth that might explain this phenomena, and I come up with an Anancy story. If the myth of the African spiderman was true, then we, the human race, were all little scattered pieces of the great shadow world.

Anancy was the man whose shadow was broken into the black mirrors of darkness. He became a spider by choice, the companion, the weaver of disparate darkness.

I ask Mackie, "Did that guy dream *me*? Or did I dream *him*?"

"Either way." Mackie explains. "Maybe both ways, same time. Maybe him just gi' a knockout from de obeah man, an him wake up in your worl'."

"Why mine?"

Mackie smiles.

"Why?"

"Them seh some mon like open book. Your book open all de while."

"So, we are all prisoners of different dreams."

"No, mon. We are all free inna de same dream. It when we wake, we haffa go prison. Unless you haffa key." He grins evasively.

"Loan me the key, Mackie."

"Yah, mon."

Glossary

ackee: A fruit/vegetable: when cooked with salt fish, this is the Jamaican national dish.

bammy: cassava cake

buckra: white overseer or just boss man

bwai *or* **bwoi:** boy

calaloo: Jamaican spinach

carry-come: to bring

cotch: to support or place temporarily

croaker lizard: Jamaican gecko

dibby-dibby: peevish or foolish

duppy: ghost

dweet: do it

Faddeh: father, sometimes used as Father, as in the Lord

fe *or* **fi:** for or to

fenky-fenky: fussy, comes from the word *finicky*

haffa: have a, or have to

higgler: street vendor

irie: good vibrations, exclamation of good feeling

ital: natural

likkle: little

macca: thorn or sticker

maga: skinny

Maroon: from the Spanish word *cimarron* or runaway; also the native population of Maroon Town, generally West African Ashanti people

mek we wait: let us wait

mosh: to mess up or mash down

nyam: to eat

ooman: woman

overstand: Rasta version of, to understand

quit: any of a number of small song birds

seen?: Do you understand what I am saying, thinking, meaning?

seen!: Yes, I understand.

Sinkle Bible: aloe plant that offers so many cures it is called a Single Bible

sulkie: (also silkie) a seal person from British Isles mythology

tek: take

turn fool: to go crazy, from Elizabethan English

unu: all of you, everyone

wiss *or* withe: common tropical vine in Jamaica

Bibliography

Adams, Emilie. *Understanding Jamaican Patois: An Introduction to Afro-Jamaican Grammar.* Kingston, Jamaica: Kingston Publishers, 1992.

Barrett, Leonard. *The Rastafarians: Sounds of Cultural Dissonance.* Boston, Mass.: Beacon Press, 1988.

Boot, Adrian, and Michael Thomas. *Jamaica: Babylon on a Thin Wire.* New York: Schocken Books, 1977.

Brooks, Lester. *Great Civilizations of Ancient Africa.* New York: Four Winds, 1971.

Cargill, Morris. *Ian Fleming Introduces Jamaica.* London: Andre Deutsche, 1965.

Cassidy, Frederic. *Jamaica Talk: 300 Hundred Years of the English Language in Jamaica.* London: Macmillan Caribbean, 1982.

Chevannes, Barry. *Rastafari: Roots and Ideology.* Syracuse, N.Y.: Syracuse U. Press, 1994.

Davis, Stephen, and Peter Simon. *Reggae Bloodlines: In Search of the Music and Culture of Jamaica.* New York: Anchor, 1979.

Drimmer, Melvin. *Black History: A Reappraisal.* Garden City, N.Y.: Doubleday, 1968.

Felton, Humphrey. *Jamaica Journal.* Kingston, Jamaica: Institute of Jamaica Archive, 1890.

Grierson, Roderick, and Stuart Munro-Hay. *The Ark of the Covenant.* London: Weidenfeld and Nicolson, 1999.

Hancock, Graham. *The Sign and the Seal.* New York: Touchstone/Simon and Schuster, 1992.

Harris, J. Rendel. *The Odes and Psalms of Solomon.* Cambridge: Cambridge University Press, 1909.

Haskins, James. *Witchcraft, Mysticism and Magic in the Black World.* New York: Doubleday, 1974.

Hatch, John. *Africa Today and Tomorrow.* New York: Praeger Inc., 1965.

Hausman, Gerald. *Duppy Talk: West Indian Tales of Mystery and Magic.* New York: Simon and Schuster Inc., 1994.

——. *The Kebra Nagast: The Lost Bible of Rastafarian Wisdom and Faith from Ethiopia and Jamaica.* New York: St. Martin's Press, 1997.

The Holy Bible: King James Version. Iowa Falls, Iowa: World Bible Publishers.

Hurston, Zora Neale. *Tell My Horse.* New York: HarperCollins, 1990.

Insight Guide to Jamaica. Englewood, N. J.: Prentice Hall, 1984.

Kebra Nagast, The Queen of Sheba and Her Only Son Menyelek. London: The Medici Society, 1922.

Owens, Joseph. *Dread: The Rastafarian in Jamaica.* Kingston, Jamaica: Sangster, 1976.

Patterson, Orlando. *The Children of Sisyphus.* London: Longman, 1964.

Ranchard, Kenneth, and Cecil Gray. *West Indian Poetry: An Anthology for Schools.* Trinidad and Jamaica: Longman, 1971.

Robertson, Diane. *Jamaican Herbs: Nutritional and Medicinal Values.* Kingston, Jamaica: Jamaican Herbs Ltd., 1986.

Senior, Olive. *A–Z of Jamaican Heritage.* Kingston, Jamaica: The Gleaner Company, 1988.

Steffens, Roger. *The World of Reggae: Treasures from Roger Steffens' Reggae Archives.* Beverly Hills, Calif.: Global Treasures, 2001.

Tafari, I. Jabulani. *A Rastafari View of Marcus Mosiah Garvey.* Kingston, Jamaica: Great Company Jamaica Ltd., 1996.

Ullendorff, Edward, translator. *My Life and Ethiopia's Progress, 1892–1937, The Autobiography of Haile Selassie I.* Chicago: Frontline Publishers, 1997.

White, Timothy. *Catch a Fire: The Life of Bob Marley.* New York: Henry Holt, 1989.

Williams, Eric. *Documents of West Indian History.* Trinidad: PNM Publishing Company, 1963.

Wilson, Donald G. *New Ships: An Anthology of West Indian Poetry for Secondary Schools.* London: Oxford University Press, 1975.

Index

Books of Related Interest

Meditations with the Navajo
Prayers, Songs, and Stories of Healing and Harmony
by Gerald Hausman

Meditations with Animals
A Native American Bestiary
by Gerald Hausman

The Universal Kabbalah
by Leonora Leet, Ph.D.

The Kabbalah of the Soul
The Transformative Psychology and Practices
of Jewish Mysticism
by Leonora Leet, Ph.D.

The Temple of Man
by R. A. Schwaller de Lubicz

Marijuana Medicine
A World Tour of the Healing and Visionary
Powers of Cannabis
by Christian Rätsch

The Temple of Solomon
From Ancient Israel to Secret Societies
by James Wasserman

The Real Name of God
Embracing the Full Essence of the Divine
by Rabbi Wayne Dosick, Ph.D.

INNER TRADITIONS • BEAR & COMPANY
P.O. Box 388
Rochester, VT 05767
1-800-246-8648
www.InnerTraditions.com

Or contact your local bookseller